HOUSE OF TASSIS

Books LLC®, Reference Series, Memphis, USA, 2011. ISBN: 9781156030424. www.booksllc.net. Copyright: http://creativecommons.org/licenses/by-sa/3.0/deed.en

Table of Contents

House of Tassis
Bernardo Tasso 2
Taxis-Bordogna-Valnigra 2
Torquato Tasso 3

House of Thurn and Taxis
Albert, 12th Prince of Thurn and Taxis 8
Albert, 8th Prince of Thurn and Taxis 9
Alessandro, 1st Duke of Castel Duino 10
Alexander Ferdinand, 3rd Prince of Thurn and Taxis 10
Anselm Franz, 2nd Prince of Thurn and Taxis 11
Archduchess Margarethe Klementine of Austria 12
Baroness Wilhelmine of Dörnberg ... 12
Carlo Alessandro, 3rd Duke of Castel Duino 13
Czech branch of the House of Thurn and Taxis 13
Duchess Auguste of Württemberg 15
Duchess Helene in Bavaria 15
Duchess Therese of Mecklenburg-Strelitz 16
Duke of Castel Duino 18
Eugen Alexander Franz, 1st Prince of Thurn and Taxis 18
Franz Joseph, 9th Prince of Thurn and Taxis 19
Fritz von Thurn und Taxis 20
Gloria, Princess of Thurn and Taxis . 20
House of Thurn and Taxis line of succession 21
Johannes, 11th Prince of Thurn and Taxis 21
Karl Alexander, 5th Prince of Thurn and Taxis 22
Karl Anselm, 4th Prince of Thurn and Taxis 23
Karl August, 10th Prince of Thurn and Taxis 24
Margravine Sophie Christine of Brandenburg-Bayreuth 24
Maria Theresia Ahlefeldt 25
Maximilian Anton Lamoral, Hereditary Prince of Thurn and Taxis 25
Maximilian Karl, 6th Prince of Thurn and Taxis 26
Maximilian Maria, 7th Prince of Thurn and Taxis 27
Order of Parfaite Amitié 28
Prince Gabriel of Thurn and Taxis 28
Prince Gustav of Thurn and Taxis 28
Prince Gustav of Thurn and Taxis (1848–1914) 29
Prince Ludwig Philipp of Thurn and Taxis 29
Prince Max Emanuel of Thurn and Taxis 30
Prince Max Emanuel of Thurn and Taxis (b. 1935) 30
Prince Paul of Thurn and Taxis 31
Princess Christa of Thurn and Taxis . 34
Princess Elisabeth Helene of Thurn and Taxis 34
Princess Elisabeth of Luxembourg (1901–1950) 35
Princess Elisabeth of Thurn and Taxis 35
Princess Elisabeth von Thurn und Taxis 36
Princess Eugénie of Greece and Denmark 36
Princess Eulalia of Thurn and Taxis . 37
Princess Iniga of Thurn and Taxis 38
Princess Isabel Maria of Braganza 38
Princess Lida of Thurn and Taxis 39
Princess Louise of Thurn and Taxis.. 41
Princess Maria Anna of Braganza..... 41
Princess Maria Augusta of Thurn and Taxis 41
Princess Maria Sophia of Thurn and Taxis 43
Princess Maria Theresia of Thurn and Taxis (1794–1874) 43
Princess Maria Theresia of Thurn and Taxis (b. 1980) 44
Princess Mathilde Sophie of Oettingen-Oettingen and Oettingen-Spielberg ... 44
Princess Sophie Friederike of Thurn and Taxis 45
Raimundo, 2nd Duke of Castel Duino 46
Thurn-und-Taxis-Post 46
Thurn und Taxis 48

Introduction

Purchase of this book entitles you to a free trial membership in the publisher's book club at www.booksllc.net. (Time limited offer.) Simply enter the barcode number from the back cover onto the membership form. The book club entitles you to select from hundreds of thousands of books at no additional charge. You can also download a digital copy of this and related books to read on the go. Simply enter the title or subject onto the search form to find them.

Each chapter in this book ends with a URL to a hyperlinked online version. Type the URL exactly as it appears. If you change the URL's capitalization it won't work. Use the online version to access related pages, websites, footnotes, tables, color photos, updates. Click the version history tab to see the chapter's contributors. Click the edit link to suggest changes.

A large and diverse editor base collaboratively wrote the book, not a single author. After a long process of discussion and debate, the chapters gradually took on a neutral point of view reached

Bernardo Tasso

Bernardo Tasso.

Bernardo Tasso (November 11, 1493 – September 5, 1569), born in Bergamo, was an Italian courtier and poet.

He was, for many years, secretary in the service of the prince of Salerno, and his wife Porzia de Rossi was closely connected with the most illustrious Neapolitan families. Their son, the great poet Torquato Tasso, was born at Sorrento in 1544.

During the boy's childhood the prince of Salerno came into collision with the Spanish government of Naples, was outlawed, and was deprived of his hereditary fiefs. Tasso shared in this disaster of his patron. He and his son were proclaimed rebels to the state.

Bernardo moved to Rome where his son joined him in about 1552. In 1556 news came that Porzia had died, and Bernardo suspected her brother of poisoning her with the object of getting control over her property. As it subsequently happened, Porzias estate never descended to her son; and the daughter Cornelia married below her birth, at the instigation of her maternal relatives.

He served various noblemen then, among them duke Guidobaldo II, in whose court his son Torquato was educated. When Bernardo was serving the duke of Milan, Guglielmo Gonzaga, he was appointed governor of Ostiblia.

When, therefore, an opening at the court of Urbino was offered in 1557, Bernardo Tasso gladly accepted it. He read cantos of his *Amadigi* to the duchess and her ladies, or discussed the merits of Homer and Virgil, Trissino and Ariosto, with the duke's librarians and secretaries. He also traveled to Venice to superintend the printing of the *Amadigi*.

Bernardo Tasso died in Ostiglia, then part of the Duchy of Mantua.

Work

An author of diverse works, Tasso wrote psalms, eclogues, sonnets and odes. The latter were the first Italian poems written in the manner of Horace. His lyric poems were published with the title *Amori* in Venice (1555). His main work, *L'Amadigi*, is an epic poem divided in 100 cantos and inspired by the Spanish chivalric romance Amadis de Gaula (known in fragmentary form since the 14th century; first printed in its entirety in 1508). The Amadigi was left incomplete but was later completed by his son Torquato, who published the full text under the title Floridante in 1587.

Source (edited): "http://en.wikipedia.org/wiki/Bernardo_Tasso"

Taxis-Bordogna-Valnigra

Taxis-Bordogna-Valnigra is the name of the descendants of *Elisabeth von Taxis* († 1518) and her husband *Bonus von Bordogna*. Elisabeth Taxis was a sister of the Brussels Postmaster General Johann Baptista of Taxis (1470–1541), the ancestor of the Princely House of Thurn and Taxis.

Family

The House of Taxis-Bordogna-Valnigra was first mentioned in documents in 1148 with Angelbertus de Fondra, and goes back to Bonazolus Fondra de Bordogna (c. 1330).

Bonus von Bordogna worked with his in-laws in the Taxis family's postal system and took over the post office in Trento from his brother-in-law David von Taxis. The next iteration of the family's surname was *Bordogna von Taxis*. Charles VI, Holy Roman Emperor elevated the Bordogna von Taxis family to the rank of barons and then later to counts under the surname *Taxis-Bordogna-Valnigra*. The baronial branch held the Lieutenant Postmaster General position in Trento and the Adige and the counts held the Lieutenant Postmaster General position in Bolzano.

The descendants of Lamoral, Baron Taxis di Bordogna e Valnigra (1900–1966) from his marriage to Princess Theresia Christiane of Saxe-Coburg and Gotha (1902–1990), daughter of Prince August Leopold of Saxe-Coburg-Kohary and his wife Archduchess Karoline Marie of Austria, are known by the family name *Tasso de Saxe-Coburgo e Bragança*.

Postmasters and Hereditary Postmaster Colonel

- Bonus de Bordogna (1482–1560), Imperial Postmaster of Trento
- Lorenz I Bordogna of Taxis (1510–1559), Imperial Postmaster of Trento

- Johann Bapitsta Bordogna of Taxis (1538–1593), Imperial Postmaster of Trento
- Lorenz II Bordogna of Taxis (1574–1612), Imperial Postmaster of Trento
- Lorenz III Bordogna of Taxis (1612–1651), Imperial Postmaster of Trento

Trento line
- Peter Paul Bordogna of Taxis (1639–1706), Imperial Postmaster of Trento
- Lorenz Anton, Baron of Taxis-Bordogna-Valnigra (1671–1744), Hereditary Postmaster Colonel (German: Obrist-Erbpostmeister) of Trento
- Johann Franz, Baron of Taxis-Bordogna-Valnigra (1724–1791), Hereditary Postmaster Colonel of Trento
- Alois Lorenz, Baron of Taxis-Bordogna-Valnigra (1750–1805), Hereditary Postmaster Colonel of Trento
- Peter Vigilius, Baron of Taxis-Bordogna-Valnigra (1780–1836), Hereditary Postmaster Colonel of Trento
- Josef Emmanuel, Baron of Taxis-Bordogna-Valnigra (1834–1886), Hereditary Postmaster Colonel of Trento

Bolzano line
- Lorenz IV Bordogna of Taxis (1651–1723), Imperial Postmaster of Bolzano
- Ferdinand Philipp, Baron of Taxis-Bordogna-Valnigra (1706–1776), Hereditary Postmaster Colonel of Bolzano
- Franz Josef, Baron of Taxis-Bordogna-Valnigra (1733–1797), Hereditary Postmaster Colonel of Bolzano
- Ägid Josef, Count of Taxis-Bordogna-Valnigra (1782–1862), Hereditary Postmaster Colonel of Bolzano, Imperial Chamberlain and Major General
- Johann Nepomuk, Count of Taxis-Bordogna-Valnigra (1833–1889), Hereditary Postmaster Colonel of Bolzano
- Johann Ägid, Count of Taxis-Bordogna-Valnigra (1856–1930), Hereditary Postmaster Colonel of Bolzano

Source (edited): "http://en.wikipedia.org/wiki/Taxis-Bordogna-Valnigra"

Torquato Tasso

Torquato Tasso (11 March 1544 – 25 April 1595) was an Italian poet of the 16th century, best known for his poem *La Gerusalemme liberata* (*Jerusalem Delivered*, 1580), in which he depicts a highly imaginative version of the combats between Christians and Muslims at the end of the First Crusade, during the siege of Jerusalem. He suffered from mental illness and died a few days before he was due to be crowned as the king of poets by the Pope. Until the beginning of the 19th century, Tasso remained one of the most widely read poets in Europe.

Biography

Early life
Born in Sorrento, he was the son of Bernardo Tasso, a nobleman of Bergamo and an epic and lyric poet of considerable fame in his day, and his wife Porzia de Rossi, a noblewoman from Tuscany. His father had for many years been secretary in the service of Ferrante Sanseverino, prince of Salerno, and his mother was closely connected with the most illustrious Neapolitan families. When the prince of Salerno came into collision with the Spanish government of Naples, was outlawed, and was deprived of his hereditary fiefs, Tasso's father shared in this his patron's fate. He was proclaimed a rebel to the state, together with his son Torquato, and his patrimony was sequestered. These things happened during the boy's childhood. In 1552 he was living with his mother and his only sister Cornelia at Naples, pursuing his education under the Jesuits, who had recently opened a school there. The precocity of intellect and the religious fervour of the boy attracted general admiration. At the age of eight he was already famous.

Soon after this date he joined his father, who then resided in great poverty, an exile and without occupation, in Rome. News reached them in 1556 that Porzia Tasso had died suddenly and mysteriously at Naples. Her husband was firmly convinced that she had been poisoned by her brother with the object of getting control over her property.

As it subsequently happened, Porzia's estate never descended to her son; and the daughter Cornelia married below her birth, at the instigation of her maternal relatives. Tasso's father was a poet by predilection and a professional courtier. Therefore, when an opening at the court of Urbino was offered in 1557, Bernardo Tasso gladly accepted it.

The young Torquato, a handsome and brilliant lad, became the companion in sports and studies of Francesco Maria della Rovere, heir to the duke of Urbino. At Urbino a society of cultivated men pursued the aesthetical and literary studies which were then in vogue. Bernardo Tasso read cantos of his Amadigi to the duchess and her ladies, or discussed the merits of Homer and Virgil, Trissino and Ariosto, with the duke's librarians and secretaries. Torquato grew up in an atmosphere of refined luxury and somewhat pedantic criticism, both of which gave a permanent tone to his character.

At Venice, where his father went to superintend the printing of his own epic, L'Amadigi (1560), these influences continued. He found himself the pet and prodigy of a distinguished literary circle. But Bernardo had suffered in his own career so seriously from dependence on the Muses and the nobility that he now determined on a lucrative profession for his son. Torquato was sent to study law at Padua. Instead of applying himself to law, the young man bestowed all his attention upon philosophy and poetry. Before the end of 1562, he had produced a narrative poem called *Rinaldo*, which was meant to combine the regularity of the Virgilian with the attractions of the romantic epic. In the attainment of this object, and in all the minor qualities of style and handling, *Rinaldo* showed such marked originality that its author was proclaimed the most promising poet of his time. The flattered father allowed it to be printed; and, after a short period of study at Bologna, he consented to his son's entering the service of Cardinal Luigi d'Este.

Castello degli Estensi, Ferrara.

France and Ferrara

In 1565, Tasso for the first time set foot in that castle at Ferrara which was destined for him to be the scene of so many glories, and such cruel sufferings. After the publication of *Rinaldo* he had expressed his views upon the epic in some *Discourses on the Art of Poetry*, which committed him to a distinct theory and gained for him the additional celebrity of a philosophical critic. The age was nothing if not critical; but it may be esteemed a misfortune for the future author of the *Gerusalemme* that he should have started with pronounced opinions upon art. Essentially a poet of impulse and instinct, he was hampered in production by his own rules.

The five years between 1565 and 1570 seem to have been the happiest of Tasso's life, although his father's death in 1569 caused his affectionate nature profound pain. Young, handsome, accomplished in all the exercises of a well-bred gentleman, accustomed to the society of the great and learned, illustrious by his published works in verse and prose, he became the idol of the most brilliant court in Italy. The first two books of his five-hundred-odd love poems were sequences addressed to Lucrezia Bendidio and Laura Peperara, court ladies and illustrious singers. The princesses Lucrezia and Leonora d'Este, both unmarried, both his seniors by about ten years, took him under their protection. He was admitted to their familiarity. He owed much to the constant kindness of both sisters. In 1570 he traveled to Paris with the cardinal.

Frankness of speech and a certain habitual want of tact caused a disagreement with his worldly patron. He left France next year, and took service under Duke Alfonso II of Ferrara. The most important events in Tasso's biography during the following four years are the publication of *Aminta* in 1573 and the completion of *Gerusalemme Liberata* in 1574. *Aminta* is a pastoral drama of very simple plot, but of exquisite lyrical charm. It appeared at the moment when music, under Palestrina's impulse, was becoming the main art of Italy. The honeyed melodies and sensuous melancholy of *Aminta* exactly suited and interpreted the spirit of its age. Its influence, in opera and cantata, was felt through two successive centuries.

The *Gerusalemme Liberata*

The *Gerusalemme Liberata* occupies a larger space in the history of European literature, and is a more considerable work. Yet the commanding qualities of this epic poem, those which revealed Tasso's individuality, and which made it immediately pass into the rank of classics, beloved by the people no less than by persons of culture, are akin to the lyrical graces of Aminta.

Its hero was Godfrey of Bouillon, the leader of the first Crusade; the climax of the epic was the capture of the holy city.

It was finished in Tasso's thirty-first year; and when the manuscripts lay before him the best part of his life was over, his best work had been already accomplished.

Troubles immediately began to gather round him. Instead of having the courage to obey his own instinct, and to publish the *Gerusalemme* as he had conceived it, he yielded to the critical scrupulosity which formed a secondary feature of his character.

The poem was sent in manuscript to several literary men of eminence, Tasso expressing his willingness to hear their strictures and to adopt their suggestions unless he could convert them to his own views. The result was that each of these candid friends, while expressing in general high admiration for the epic, took some exception to its plot, its title, its moral tone, its episodes or its diction, in detail. One wished it to be more regularly classical; another wanted more romance. One hinted that the Inquisition would not tolerate its supernatural machinery; another demanded the excision of its most charming passages, the loves of *Armida*, *Clorinda* and *Erminia*. Tasso had to defend himself against all these ineptitudes and pedantries, and to accommodate his practice to the theories he had rashly expressed.

As in the *Rinaldo*, so also in the *Jerusalem Delivered*, he aimed at ennobling the Italian epic style by preserving strict unity of plot and heightening poetic diction. He chose Virgil for his model, took the first crusade for subject, infused the fervour of religion into his conception of the hero *Godfrey*. But his natural bias was for romance.

In spite of the poet's ingenuity and industry the stately main theme evinced less spontaneity of genius than the romantic episodes with which he adorned it, as he had done in Rinaldo. *Godfrey*, a mixture of pious Aeneas and Tridentine Catholicism, is not the real hero of the *Gerusalemme*. Fiery and passionate *Rinaldo*, *Ruggiero*, melancholy impulsive *Tancredi*, and the chivalrous Saracens with whom they clash in love and war, divide the reader's interest and divert it from *Goffredo*.

The action of the epic turns on *Armida*, the beautiful witch, sent forth by the infernal senate to sow discord in the Christian camp. She is converted to the true faith by her adoration for a crusading knight, and quits the scene with a phrase of the Virgin Mary on her lips. Brave *Clorinda* dons armour like

Marfisa, fighting in a duel with her devoted lover and receiving baptism from his hands at the time of her pathetic death; *Erminia* seeks refuge in the shepherds' hut. These lovely pagan women, so touching in their sorrows, so romantic in their adventures, so tender in their emotions, rivet the readers' attention, while the battles, religious ceremonies, conclaves and stratagems of the campaign are easily skipped. The truth is that Tasso's great invention as an artist was the poetry of sentiment. Sentiment, not sentimentality, gives value to what is immortal in the *Gerusalemme*. It was a new thing in the 16th century, something concordant with a growing feeling for woman and with the ascendant art of music. This sentiment, refined, noble, natural, steeped in melancholy, exquisitely graceful, pathetically touching, breathes throughout the episodes of the *Gerusalemme*, finds metrical expression in the languishing cadence of its mellifluous verse, and sustains the ideal life of those seductive heroines whose names were familiar as household words to all Europe in the 17th and 18th centuries.

Tasso's self-chosen critics were not men to admit what the public has since accepted as incontrovertible. They vaguely felt that a great and beautiful romantic poem was imbedded in a dull and not very correct epic. In their uneasiness they suggested every course but the right one, which was to publish the *Gerusalemme* without further dispute.

Tasso, already overworked by his precocious studies, by exciting court-life and exhausting literary industry, now grew almost mad with worry. His health began to fail him. He complained of headache, suffered from malarious fevers, and wished to leave Ferrara. The *Gerusalemme* was laid in manuscript upon a shelf. He opened negotiations with the court of Florence for an exchange of service. This irritated the duke of Ferrara. Alfonso hated nothing more than to see courtiers leave him for a rival duchy.

Difficult relationships in the Court of Ferrara

Alfonso II d'Este, portrait by Girolamo da Carpi.

Alfonso thought, moreover, that, if Tasso were allowed to go, the Medici would get the coveted dedication of that already famous epic. Therefore he bore with the poet's humours, and so contrived that the latter should have no excuse for quitting Ferrara. Meanwhile, through the years 1575, 1576 and 1577, Tasso's health grew worse.

Jealousy inspired the courtiers to malign and insult him. His irritable and suspicious temper, vain and sensitive to slights, rendered him only too easy a prey to their malevolence.

In the 1570s Tasso developed a persecution mania which led to legends about the restless, half-mad, and misunderstood author.

He became consumed by thoughts that his servants betrayed his confidence, fancied he had been denounced to the Inquisition, and expected daily to be poisoned. Literary and political events surrounding him contributed to upsets and the mental state, with troubles, stress and social troubles escalating.

In the autumn of 1576 Tasso quarrelled with a Ferrarese gentleman, Maddalo, who had talked too freely about some same-sex love affair; the same year he wrote a letter to his homosexual friend Luca Scalabrino dealing with his own love for a twenty-one year old young man Orazio Ariosto; in the summer of 1577 he drew his knife upon a servant in the presence of Lucrezia d'Este, duchess of Urbino. For this excess he was arrested; but the duke released him, and took him for a change of air to his country seat of Belriguardo. What happened there is not known.

Some biographers have surmised that a compromising liaison with Leonora d'Este came to light, and that Tasso agreed to feign madness in order to cover her honor, but of this there is no proof. It is only certain that from Belriguardo he returned to a Franciscan convent at Ferrara, for the express purpose of attending to his health. There the dread of being murdered by the duke took firm hold on his mind. He escaped at the end of July, disguised himself as a peasant, and went on foot to his sister at Sorrento.

The conclusions were that Tasso, after the beginning of 1575, became the victim of a mental malady, which, without amounting to actual insanity, rendered him fantastical and insupportable, a cause of anxiety to his patrons.

There is no evidence whatsoever that this state of things was due to an overwhelming passion for Leonora. The duke, contrary to his image as a tyrant, showed considerable forbearance. He was a rigid and not sympathetic man, as egotistical as a princeling of that age was wont to be. But to Tasso he was never cruel; unintelligent perhaps, but far from being that monster of ferocity which has been painted. The subsequent history of his connection with the poet corroborates this view.

While at Sorrento, Tasso yearned for Ferrara. The court-made man could not breathe freely outside its charmed circle. He wrote humbly requesting to be taken back. Alfonso consented, provided Tasso would agree to undergo a medical course of treatment for his melancholy. When he returned, which he did with alacrity under those conditions, he was well received by the ducal family.

All might have gone well if his old maladies had not revived. Scene followed scene of irritability, moodiness, suspicion, wounded vanity and violent outbursts.

In the madhouse of St. Anna

In the summer of 1578 he ran away again; travelled through Mantua, Padua, Venice, Urbino, Lombardy. In September he reached the gates of Turin on foot, and was courteously entertained by Emmanuel Philibert, Duke of Savoy. Wherever he went, wandering like the world's rejected guest, he met with the honour due to his illustrious name. Great folk opened their houses to him gladly, partly in compassion, partly in admiration of his genius. But he soon wearied of their society, and wore their kindness thin by his querulous peevishness. It seemed, moreover, that life was intolerable to him outside Ferrara. Accordingly he once more opened negotiations with the duke; and in February 1579 he again set foot in the castle.

Alfonso was about to contract his third marriage, this time with a princess of the house of Mantua. He had no children, and unless he got an heir, there was a probability that his state would fall, as it did subsequently, to the Holy See. The nuptial festivals, on the eve of which Tasso arrived, were not therefore an occasion of great rejoicing for the elderly bridegroom. As a forlorn hope he had to wed a third wife; but his heart was not engaged and his expectations were far from sanguine.

Tasso, preoccupied as always with his own sorrows and his own sense of dignity, made no allowance for the troubles of his master. Rooms below his rank, he thought, had been assigned him; the Duke was engaged. Without exercising common patience, or giving his old friends the benefit of a doubt, he broke into terms of open abuse, behaved like a lunatic, and was sent off without ceremony to the madhouse of St. Anna. This happened in March 1579; and there he remained until July 1586. Duke Alfonso's long-sufferance at last had given way. He firmly believed that Tasso was insane, and he felt that if he were so St. Anna was the safest place for him. Tasso had put himself in the wrong by his intemperate conduct, but far more by that incomprehensible yearning after the Ferrarese court which made him return to it again and yet again.

"Tasso in the Hospital of St Anna at Ferrara" by Eugène Delacroix. Tasso spent 1579-1586 in the madhouse of St Anne.

It was no doubt very irksome for a man of Tasso's pleasure-loving, restless and self-conscious spirit to be kept for more than seven years in confinement. Yet one must weigh the facts of the case rather than the fancies which have been indulged regarding them. After the first few months of his incarceration he obtained spacious apartments, received the visits of friends, went abroad attended by responsible persons of his acquaintance, and corresponded freely with whomsoever he chose to address. The letters written from St. Anna to the princes and cities of Italy, to warm well-wishers, and to men of the highest reputation in the world of art and learning, form the most valuable source of information, not only on his then condition, but also on his temperament at large. It is singular that he spoke always respectfully, even affectionately, of the Duke.

Some critics have attempted to make it appear that he was hypocritically kissing the hand which had chastised him, with the view of being released from prison, but no one who has impartially considered the whole tone and tenor of his epistles will adopt this opinion. What emerges clearly from them is that he labored under a serious mental disease, and that he was conscious of it.

Meanwhile, he occupied his uneasy leisure with copious compositions. The mass of his prose dialogues on philosophical and ethical themes, which is very considerable, belong to the years of imprisonment in St. Anna.

Except for occasional odes or sonnets—some written at request and only rhetorically interesting, a few inspired by his keen sense of suffering and therefore poignant—he neglected poetry. But everything which fell from his pen during this period was carefully preserved by the Italians, who, while they regarded him as a lunatic, somewhat illogically scrambled for the very offscourings of his wit.

Nor can it be said that society was wrong. Tasso had proved himself an impracticable human being; but he remained a man of genius, the most interesting personality in Italy.

Long ago his papers had been sequestered. In the year 1580, he heard that part of the *Gerusalemme* was being published without his permission and without his corrections. The following year, the whole poem was given to the world, and in the following six months seven editions issued from the press.

The prisoner of St. Anna had no control over his editors; and from the masterpiece which placed him on the level of Petrarch and Ariosto he never derived one penny of pecuniary profit. A rival poet at the court of Ferrara undertook to revise and edit his lyrics in 1582. This was Battista Guarini; and Tasso, in his cell, had to allow odes and sonnets, poems of personal feeling, occasional pieces of compliment, to be collected and emended, without lifting a voice in the matter.

A few years later, in 1585, two Florentine pedants of the Crusca Academy declared war against the *Gerusalemme*. They loaded it with insults, which seem to those who read their pamphlets now mere parodies of criticism. Yet Tasso felt bound to reply; and he did so with a moderation and urbanity which prove him to have been not only in full possession of his reasoning faculties, but a gentleman of noble manners also. The man, like Hamlet, was distraught through ill-accommodation to his circumstances and his age; brain-sick he was undoubtedly; and this is the Duke of Ferrara's justification for the treatment he endured. In the prison he bore himself pathetically, peevishly, but never ignobly. He showed a singular indifference to the fate of his great poem, a rare magnanimity in dealing with its detractors. His own personal distress, that terrible malaise of imperfect insanity, absorbed him.

What remained over, untouched by the malady, unoppressed by his consciousness thereof, displayed a sweet and gravely-toned humanity. The oddest thing about his life in prison is that he was always trying to place his two nephews, the sons of his sister Cornelia, in court-service. One of them he attached to Guglielmo I, Duke of Mantua, the other to Ottavio Farnese, Duke of Parma.

After all his father's and his own lessons of life, he had not learned that the court was to be shunned like Circe by an honest man. In estimating Duke Alfonso's share of blame, this wilful idealization of the court by Tasso must be taken into account. That man is not a tyrant's victim who moves heaven and earth to place his sister's sons with tyrants.

Late years

In 1586 Tasso left St. Anna at the solicitation of Vincenzo Gonzaga, Prince of Mantua. He followed his young deliverer to the city by the Mincio, basked awhile in liberty and courtly pleasures, enjoyed a splendid reception from his paternal town of Bergamo, and produced a meritorious tragedy called *Torrismondo*. But only a few months had passed when he grew discontented. Vincenzo Gonzaga, succeeding to his father's dukedom of Mantua, had scanty leisure to bestow upon the poet. Tasso felt neglected. In the autumn of 1587 he journeyed through Bologna and Loreto to Rome, and taking up his quarters there with an old friend, Scipione Gonzaga, now Patriarch of Jerusalem. Next year he wandered off to Naples, where he wrote a dull poem on Monte Oliveto. In 1589 he returned to Rome, and took up his quarters again with the patriarch of Jerusalem. The servants found him insufferable, and turned him out of doors. He fell ill, and went to a hospital. The patriarch in 1590 again received him. But Tasso's restless spirit drove him forth to Florence. The Florentines said, "Actum est de eo." Rome once more, then Mantua, then Florence, then Rome, then Naples, then Rome, then Naples—such is the weary record of the years 1590-94. He endured a veritable Odyssey of malady, indigence and misfortune. To Tasso everything came amiss. He had the palaces of princes, cardinals, patriarchs, nay popes, always open to him. Yet he could rest in none. Gradually, in spite of all veneration for the *sacer vates*, he made himself the laughingstock and bore of Italy.

His health grew ever feebler and his genius dimmer. In 1592, he gave to the public a revised version of the *Gerusalemme*. It was called the *Gerusalemme Conquistata*. All that made the poem of his early manhood charming he rigidly erased. The versification was degraded; the heavier elements of the plot underwent a dull rhetorical development. During the same year a prosaic composition in Italian blank verse, called *Le Sette Giornate*, saw the light. Nobody reads it now. It is only mentioned as one of Tasso's dotages—a dreary amplification of the first chapter of Genesis.

It is singular that just in these years, when mental disorder, physical weakness, and decay of inspiration seemed dooming Tasso to oblivion, his old age was cheered with brighter rays of hope. Pope Clement VIII ascended the papal chair in 1592. He and his nephew, Cardinal Aldobrandini of San Giorgio, determined to befriend the poet. In 1594, they invited him to Rome. There he was to receive the crown of laurels, as Petrarch had been crowned, on the Capitol.

Worn out with illness, Tasso reached Rome in November. The ceremony of his coronation was deferred because Cardinal Aldobrandini had fallen ill, but the pope assigned him a pension; and, under the pressure of pontifical remonstrance, Prince Avellino, who held Tasso's maternal estate, agreed to discharge a portion of his claims by payment of a yearly rent-charge.

At no time since Tasso left St. Anna had the heavens apparently so smiled upon him. Capitolian honors and money were now at his disposal. Yet fortune came too late. Before he wore the crown of poet laureate, or received his pensions, he ascended to the convent of Sant'Onofrio, on a stormy 1 April 1595. Seeing a cardinal's coach toil up the steep Trasteverine Hill, the monks came to the door to greet it. From the carriage stepped Tasso and told the prior he had come to die with him.

He died in Sant'Onofrio in April 1595. He was just past fifty-one; and the last twenty years of his existence had been practically and artistically ineffectual.

At the age of thirty-one the *Gerusalemme*, was accomplished. The world too was already ringing with the music of *Aminta*. More than this Tasso had naught to give to literature but those succeeding years of derangement, exile, imprisonment, poverty and hope deferred endear the man to readers. Elegiac and querulous as he must always appear, Tasso was loved better in the Romantic period because he suffered through nearly a quarter of a century of slow decline and unexplained misfortune.

Other works

Rime (Rhymes), nearly two thousand lyrics in nine books, were written between 1567 and 1593. Influenced by Petrarca's Canzoniere, they develop a research for musicality and are rich of delicate images and subtle sentiments.

Galealto re di Norvegia, (1573-4) an unfinished tragedy, which later was finished with a new title: *Re Torrismondo* (1587). It is influenced by Sophocles's and Seneca's tragedies, and tells the story of princess Alvida of Norway, who is forcibly married off to the Goth king Torrismondo, when she is devoted to her childhood friend, king Germondo of Sweden.

Dialoghi (Dialogues), written between 1578 and 1594. These 28 texts deal with various issues, from moral ones (love, virtue, nobility) to more mundane ones (masks, play, courtly style, beauty). Sometimes Tasso touches major themes of his time: for instance, religion vs. intellectual freedom; Christianity vs. Islam at Lepanto.

Discorsi del poema eroico, published in 1594. This is the main text to understand Tasso's poetics and was probably written during the long years or composing and revising *Gerusalemme Liberata*

The disease

The Convent of Sant'Onofrio.

The disease Tasso began to suffer from is now believed to be schizophrenia. Legends describe him wandering the streets of Rome half mad, convinced that he was being persecuted. At times he was imprisoned for his own safety by the Duke in St. Anne's lunatic asylum. Though he was never fully cured, he was able to function and resumed his writing. The *Gerusalemme* was published by his friends Angelo Ingegneri and Febo Bonna, mostly with the consent of the poet.

Tasso and other artists

- Tasso's lyric poetry may have had some influence in late-Renaissance France on Desportes and Ronsard (whom Tasso met in Paris). It almost certainly influenced a number of English Elizabethans, including Sir Philip Sidney, Abraham Fraunce, and Samuel Daniel.
- Claudio Monteverdi composed *Combattimento di Tancredi e Clorinda* upon the text of *Gerusalemme Liberata*, canto XII. He also composed music over some of Tasso's Rime, particularly madrigals.
- Giaches de Wert and Carlo Gesualdo da Venosa put into music many texts from Tasso's *Rime* and *Gerusalemme*.
- The German writer Johann Wolfgang von Goethe wrote a play *Torquato Tasso* in 1790, which explores the struggles of the artist. He also composed a cantata text, "Rinaldo", inspired by Canto Sixteen of "Jerusalem Delivered," which was later set to music by Johannes Brahms.
- Giacomo Leopardi wrote *Dialogo di Torquato Tasso e del suo Genio familiare* (*Operette morali*, 1824), a prose about the long stay in St. Anna. The main theme is a comparison between pain and boredom, expressed in a dialogue between Tasso and a "Genius", or ghost, said to be visiting him in his loneliness.
- Among the numerous operas based on "Jerusalem Delivered" are works by Lully, Alessandro Scarlatti, Vivaldi, Handel, Haydn, Salieri, Cherubini, Christoph Willibald Gluck, Rossini, and Dvořák. There is even an experimental modern opera on the theme, by Judith Weir, transposing the scene into contemporary Iraq.
- Both Edmund Spenser and John Milton were greatly influenced by Tasso's work.
- Lord Byron's poem "The Lament of Tasso" narrates Tasso's spell in St. Anna's hospital.
- The Italian composer Gaetano Donizetti wrote an opera on the subject of *Torquato Tasso* (1833) and incorporated some of the poet's writing into the libretto.
- Franz Liszt composed a symphonic poem, *Tasso, Lamento e Trionfo* in commemoration of the centenary of Goethe's play. The sombre first half represents his anguish in the asylum, and the glorious second half charts the acknowledgement he and his poetry achieved after he departed from the hospital.
- Artists inspired by both "Jerusalem Delivered" and "Aminta" have been legion and include Tintoretto, the Carracci, Guercino, Pietro da Cortona, Domenichino, Cigoli, Van Dyck, Poussin, Claude Lorrain, Tiepolo, Boucher, Fragonard, Johann Friedrich Overbeck, Hayez, and Delacroix.

English translations

During the Renaissance, the first (incomplete) translation of "Jerusalem Delivered" was brought out by Thomas Carew (1594). A complete version by Edward Fairfax appeared under the title "Godfrey of Bouillon" in 1600. John Hoole's version in heroic couplets followed in 1772, and Jeremiah Holmes Wiffen's (in Spenserian stanzas) in 1821. There were several twentieth century versions, including by Anthony Esolen (2000) and by Max Wickert, published as "The Liberation of Jerusalem" by Oxford University Press (2009). "Aminta", some of the "Dialogues", "Torrismondo" and some of the late religious works have also been issued in English.

Source (edited): "http://en.wikipedia.org/wiki/Torquato_Tasso"

Albert, 12th Prince of Thurn and Taxis

Albert Maria Lamoral Miguel Johannes Gabriel, 12th Prince of Thurn and Taxis, or legally **Albert Prinz von Thurn und Taxis**, (born 24 June 1983, Regensburg, Bavaria, Germany) is a German prince and socialite. He has been listed as the world's youngest billionaire many times since his father's death in 1990. He first appeared on the list when he was age eight. His mother, Princess Gloria (née Countess of Schönburg in Glauchau and Waldenburg), was a popular media figure in the 1980s, and was instrumental in preserving his fortune until he was old enough to officially inherit it. He has two older sisters: Princess Maria Theresia and Princess Elisabeth.

Biography

Education

Prince Albert completed his high school education in Rome and then, after his military service, he went to the University of Edinburgh where he studied economics and theology. He is an enthusiastic racing driver, vice-champion of the 2007 German GT Championship ADAC GT Masters with the German Team Reiter Engineering.

Family

The Princely House of Thurn und Taxis is a German family whose fortune derives from their position as hereditary general postmasters of the Holy Roman Empire. As such, the family was a key player in the postal services in Europe in the 16th century. The Thurn and Taxis family remains well known as owners of breweries and builders of countless castles.

Media attention

In 2008 he was included as 11th on the list of the "20 Hottest Young Royals" as compiled by *Forbes* magazine.

As royal titles are not recognized by the German law since they were declared void in 1919, the family has included the title as an integral part of their name in the form of *Prinz von Thurn und Taxis*. Because of this the legal name of Albert is *Albert Prinz von Thurn und Taxis*, although he himself as the head of the family would be called *Albert **Fürst** von Thurn und Taxis* if his titles were legally recognized by the German state.

Titles and styles

- **24 June 1983 – 14 December 1990**: *His Serene Highness* The Hereditary Prince of Thurn and Taxis
- **14 December 1990 – present**: *His Serene Highness* The Prince of Thurn and Taxis

Honours

- Grand Master of the Order of Parfaite Amitié

Source (edited): "http://en.wikipedia.org/wiki/Albert_12th_Prince_of_Thurn_and_Taxis"

Albert, 8th Prince of Thurn and Taxis

Albert **Maria Joseph Maximilian Lamoral, Prince of Thurn and Taxis**, full German name: *Albert Maria Joseph Maximilian Lamoral Fürst von Thurn und Taxis* (born 8 May 1867 in Regensburg, Kingdom of Bavaria; died 22 January 1952 in Regensburg, Bavaria, Germany) was the eighth Prince of Thurn and Taxis and Head of the Princely House of Thurn and Taxis from 2 June 1885 until his death on 22 January 1952.

Early life

Albert was born at Regensburg, Germany, the younger son of Maximilian Anton Lamoral, Hereditary Prince of Thurn and Taxis (1831-1867) and Duchess Helene in Bavaria (1834-1890). His father died when he was less than two months old, and he was raised by his mother.

Succession

In 1871 Albert's grandfather Maximilian Karl died, and his older brother Maximilian Maria succeeded as Fürst. Maxmilian died 2 June 1885 and Albert succeeded as Fürst; his mother served as regent until his 21st birthday in 1888. On 8 May 1889 he was named Duke of Wörth and Donaustauf by Luitpold, Prince Regent of Bavaria. On 30 November 1889 he was made a knight of the Austrian Order of the Golden Fleece.

Marriage and issue

On 15 July 1890 in Budapest, Hungary, Albert married Archduchess Margarethe Klementine of Austria (6 July 1870 – 2 May 1955), daughter of Archduke Joseph Karl of Austria. Albert and Margarethe had eight children:

- Franz Joseph, 9th Prince of Thurn and Taxis (21 December 1893 – 13 July 1971), married Princess Isabel Maria of Braganza, daughter of Miguel, Duke of Braganza
- Prince Joseph Albert of Thurn and Taxis (4 November 1895 – 7 December 1895)
- Karl August, 10th Prince of Thurn and Taxis (23 July 1898 – 26 April 1982), married Princess Maria Anna of Braganza, daughter of Miguel, Duke of Braganza
- Prince Ludwig Philipp of Thurn and Taxis (2 February 1901 – 22 April 1933), married Princess Elisabeth of Luxembourg, daughter of Grand Duke William IV of Luxembourg
- Prince Max Emanuel of Thurn and Taxis (1 March 1902 – 3 October 1994)
- Princess Elisabeth Helene of Thurn and Taxis (15 December 1903 – 22 October 1976), married Friedrich Christian, Margrave of Meissen
- Prince Raphael Rainer of Thurn and Taxis (30 May 1906 – 8 June 1993), married Princess Margarete of Thurn and Taxis; father of Prince Max Emanuel of Thurn and Taxis, the current heir presumptive to Thurn and Taxis.
- Prince Philipp Ernst of Thurn and Taxis (7 May 1908 – 23 July 1964), married Princess Eulalia of Thurn and Taxis

Albert died at Regensburg where he is buried with his wife in the crypt chapel of Schloss St. Emmeram, formerly St. Emmeram's Abbey.

Titles, styles, honours and arms

Titles and styles

- **8 May 1867 – 10 November 1870**: *His Serene Highness* Prince Albert of Thurn and Taxis
- **10 November 1870 – 2 June 1885**: *His Serene Highness* The Hereditary

- Prince of Thurn and Taxis
- **2 June 1885 – 22 January 1952**: *His Serene Highness* The Prince of Thurn and Taxis

Honours
- Grand Master of the Order of Parfaite Amitié
- Knight of the Austrian Order of the Golden Fleece
- In 1923 Albert received an honorary doctorate of philosophy from the University of Innsbruck.

Source (edited): "http://en.wikipedia.org/wiki/Albert,_8th_Prince_of_Thurn_and_Taxis"

Alessandro, 1st Duke of Castel Duino

Prince Alessandro della Torre e Tasso, 1st Duke of Castel Duino, full German name: *Alexander Karl Egon Theobald Lamoral Johann Baptist Maria, Prinz von Thurn und Taxis* (born 8 July 1881 at Schloss Mzell in Mzell, Kingdom of Bohemia, Austria–Hungary; died 11 March 1937 at Castel Duino in Duino, Kingdom of Italy) was a Prince of Thurn of Taxis and a member of the Bohemian line of the Princely House of Thurn and Taxis. Alessandro was created a Prince della Torre e Tasso and first Duke of Castel Duino by Victor Emmanuel III of Italy after relocating to the Kingdom of Italy in 1923.

Family

Alessandro was the third child and son of Prince Alexander Johann of Thurn and Taxis and his wife Princess Marie of Hohenlohe-Waldenburg-Schillingsfürst. He was a great-great-great-grandson of Alexander Ferdinand, 3rd Prince of Thurn and Taxis and his wife Princess Maria Henriette Josepha of Fürstenberg-Stühlingen.

Marriage and issue

Alessandro married first to Princess Marie of Ligne, daughter of Louis, 9th Prince of Ligne and his wife Elisabeth de la Rochefoucauld, civilly on 27 January 1906 and religiously on 29 January 1906 in Paris. Alessandro and Marie had three children together:
- Prince Raimundo della Torre e Tasso, 2nd Duke of Castel Duino (Castel Duino 16 March 1907 – Castel Duino 17 March 1986), married Princess Eugénie of Greece and Denmark
- Prince Ludwig della Torre e Tasso (Castel Duino 5 October 1908 – Camillus, New York 25 March 1985), married Frances Goodyear
- Princess Margarete of Thurn and Taxis (born at Château de Belœil on 8 November 1909), married Prince Gaetan of Bourbon-Parma

Alessandro and Marie divorced in 1919. Alessandro married secondly to Helena Holbrook-Walker in 1932 in Vrana.

Titles, styles, honours and arms

Titles and styles
- **8 July 1881 – 1923**: *His Serene Highness* Prince Alexander of Thurn and Taxis
- **1923 – 11 March 1937**: *His Serene Highness* The Duke of Castel Duino, Prince della Torre e Tasso

Source (edited): "http://en.wikipedia.org/wiki/Alessandro,_1st_Duke_of_Castel_Duino"

Alexander Ferdinand, 3rd Prince of Thurn and Taxis

Alexander Ferdinand, **Prince of Thurn and Taxis**, full German name: *Alexander Ferdinand Fürst von Thurn und Taxis* (born 21 March 1704 in Frankfurt am Main, Free Imperial City of Frankfurt, Holy Roman Empire; died 17 March 1773 in Regensburg, Free Imperial City of Regensburg, Holy Roman Empire) was the third Prince of Thurn and Taxis, Postmaster General of the Imperial Reichspost, and Head of the Princely House of Thurn and Taxis from 8 November 1739 until his death on 17 March 1773. Karl Anselm served as *Prinzipalkommissar* (German: *Principal Commissioner*) at the *Immerwährender Reichstag* (German: *Perpetual Imperial Diet*) in Frankfurt am Main and Regensburg for Charles VII, Holy Roman Emperor, Francis I, Holy Roman Emperor, and Joseph II, Holy Roman Emperor from 1 February 1743 to 1745 and again from 1748 until 1773.

Early life

Alexander Ferdinand was the eldest child and only son of Anselm Franz, 2nd Prince of Thurn and Taxis and his wife Maria Ludovika Anna Franziska, Princess of Lobkowicz.

Principal Commissioner

From 1 February 1743 to 1745, Alexander Ferdinand served as Principal Commissioner for Charles VII, Holy Roman Emperor at the Perpetual Imperial Diet in Frankfurt am Main. When the Diet relocated to Regensburg under Francis I, Holy Roman Emperor, Alexander Ferdinand was reinstated as Principal Commissioner in 1748. It was for this reason that Alexander Ferdinand moved the principal residence of the Princely House of Thurn and Taxis from Frankfurt am Main to Regensburg. On 30 May 1754, Alexander Ferdinand was added to the Prince Imperial College.

Marriages and family

A proposed bride was Johanna of Baden-Baden (1704-1726), only surviving daughter of the late Margrave of Baden-Baden and his wife (Regent of Baden-Baden from 1707) Sibylle of

Saxe-Lauenburg but the match never materialised.

Alexander Ferdinand married Margravine Sophie Christine of Brandenburg-Bayreuth, eldest daughter of George Frederick Charles, Margrave of Brandenburg-Bayreuth and his wife Princess Dorothea of Schleswig-Holstein-Sonderburg-Beck, on 11 April 1731 in Frankfurt am Main. Alexander Ferdinand and Sophie Christine had five children:
- Princess Sophie Christine of Thurn and Taxis (baptized 8 December 1731 † 23 December 1731)
- Karl Anselm, 4th Prince of Thurn and Taxis (born 2 June 1733 † 13 November 1805)

∞ 3 September 1753 Duchess Auguste of Württemberg (30 October 1734-4 June 1787)

∞ 1787 Elisabeth Hildebrand, Frau von Train
- Princess Luise Auguste Charlotte of Thurn and Taxis (born 27 October 1734 † January 1735)
- Prince Friedrich August of Thurn and Taxis (baptized 5 December 1736 † 12 September 1755)
- Prince Ludwig Franz Karl Lamoral Joseph of Thurn and Taxis (born 13 October 1737 † 7 August 1738)

Alexander Ferdinand married secondly to **Louise de Lorraine**, third eldest daughter of Louis II of Lorraine-Brionne, Prince of Lambesc and his wife Jeanne Henriette de Durfort, on 22 March 1745 in Paris.

Alexander Ferdinand married thirdly to Princess Maria Henriette Josepha of Fürstenberg-Stühlingen, daughter of Joseph William Ernest, Prince of Fürstenberg-Fürstenberg and his wife Countess Theresia Anna Maria Eleanore of Waldstein, on 21 September 1750 in Regensburg. Alexander Ferdinand and Maria Henriette Josepha had seven children:
- Princess Maria Theresia of Thurn and Taxis (born 16 January 1755 † 20 December 1810)

∞ 20 August 1780 Ferdinand, Count of Ahlefeldt-Langeland
- Princess Josephine of Thurn and Taxis (born 1 August 1759 † young age)
- Prince Heinrich Alexander of Thurn and Taxis (baptized 14 September 1762 † young age)
- Prince Franz Joseph of Thurn and Taxis (born 2 October 1764; buried 20 February 1765)
- Princess Maria Anna Josepha of Thurn and Taxis (baptized 28 Sep 1766 † 10 August 1805)
- Princess Marie Elisabetha Alexandrina of Thurn and Taxis (born 30 November 1767 † 21 July 1822)

∞ 4 November 1790 Karl Joseph, Landgrave of Fürstenberg (26 June 1760-25 March 1799)

∞ Joseph, Baron of Lasaberg (died 15 March 1855)
- Prince Maximilian Joseph of Thurn and Taxis (born 9 May 1769 † 15 May 1831)

∞ 6 June 1791 Princess Eleonore of Lobkowicz (22 April 1770-9 November 1834)

from this marriage the Czech branch of the House of Thurn and Taxis descends

Titles and styles
- **21 March 1704 – 8 November 1739**: *His Serene Highness* The Hereditary Prince of Thurn and Taxis
- **8 November 1739 – 17 March 1773**: *His Serene Highness* The Prince of Thurn and Taxis

Honours
- Grand Master of the Order of Parfaite Amitié
- Knight of the Austrian Order of the Golden Fleece

Source (edited): "http://en.wikipedia.org/wiki/Alexander_Ferdinand,_3rd_Prince_of_Thurn_and_Taxis"

Anselm Franz, 2nd Prince of Thurn and Taxis

Anselm Franz, **Prince of Thurn and Taxis**, full German name: *Anselm Franz Fürst von Thurn und Taxis* (born 30 January 1681 in Brussels, Spanish Netherlands; died 8 November 1739 in Brussels, Austrian Netherlands) was the second Prince of Thurn and Taxis, Postmaster General of the Imperial Reichspost, and Head of the House of Thurn and Taxis from 21 February 1714 until his death on 8 November 1739.

Early life

Anselm Franz was the eldest child and son of Eugen Alexander Franz, 1st Prince of Thurn and Taxis and his wife Princess Anna Adelheid of Fürstenberg-Heiligenberg. The date of his birth is unknown, but Anselm Franz was baptised on 30 January 1681 at Notre-Dame du Sablon in Brussels.

Postmaster General

After assuming the position of Postmaster General of the Imperial Reichspost during the War of the Spanish Succession, Anselm Franz moved the headquarters of the Reichspost from Brussels to Frankfurt am Main. In 1725, he was able to lease the postal system of the Austrian Netherlands as a Habsburg fief. In Frankfurt, Anselm Franz began construction of the Baroque Palais Thurn und Taxis in 1729.

Marriages and family

Anselm Franz married Maria Ludovika Anna Franziska, Princess of Lobkowicz, daughter of Ferdinand August Leopold, Prince of Lobkowicz, Duke of Sagan and his wife Margravine Maria Anna Wilhelmine of Baden-Baden, on 10 January 1703. Franz Anselm and Maria Ludovika had four children:
- Alexander Ferdinand, 3rd Prince of Thurn and Taxis (1704-1773)
- Princess Philippine Eleonore Maria of Thurn and Taxis (1705-1706)
- Princess Maria Augusta of Thurn and Taxis (1706-1756)
- Prince Christian Adam Egon of Thurn and Taxis (1710-1745)

Titles and styles

- **1681 – 1695**: *His Serene Highness* The Hereditary Count of Thurn and Taxis
- **1695 – 21 February 1714**: *His Serene Highness* The Hereditary Prince of Thurn and Taxis
- **21 February 1714 – 8 November 1739**: *His Serene Highness* The Prince of Thurn and Taxis

Honours

- Knight of the Austrian Order of the Golden Fleece

Source (edited): "http://en.wikipedia.org/wiki/Anselm_Franz,_2nd_Prince_of_Thurn_and_Taxis"

Archduchess Margarethe Klementine of Austria

Archduchess Margarethe Klementine Maria of Austria (in German: *Margarethe Klementine Maria, Erzherzogin von Österreich*; in Hungarian: *Habsburg–Toscanai Margit Klementina Mária főhercegnő*; 6 July 1870, Alcsút, Austria-Hungary– 2 May 1955, Regensburg) was a member of the Hungarian line of the House of Habsburg-Lorraine and an Archduchess of Austria and Princess of Bohemia, Hungary, and Tuscany by birth. Through her marriage to Albert, 8th Prince of Thurn and Taxis, Margarethe Klementine was also a member of the House of Thurn and Taxis.

Family

Margarethe Klementine was the third-eldest daughter and child of Archduke Joseph Karl of Austria and his wife Princess Clotilde of Saxe-Coburg and Gotha. Through her father Joseph Karl, Margarethe Klementine was the great-granddaughter of Leopold II, Holy Roman Emperor. Through her mother, she was the great-granddaughter of Louis-Philippe d'Orléans, King of the French.

Life

Marriage and issue

Margarethe Klementine married Albert, 8th Prince of Thurn and Taxis, younger son of Maximilian Anton Lamoral, Hereditary Prince of Thurn and Taxis and his wife Duchess Helene in Bavaria, on 15 July 1890 in Budapest, Austria–Hungary. Margarethe Klementine and Albert had eight children:

- Franz Joseph, 9th Prince of Thurn and Taxis (21 December 1893 – 13 July 1971), married Princess Isabel Maria of Braganza, daughter of Miguel, Duke of Braganza
- Prince Joseph Albert of Thurn and Taxis (4 November 1895 – 7 December 1895)
- Karl August, 10th Prince of Thurn and Taxis (23 July 1898 – 26 April 1982), married Princess Maria Anna of Braganza, daughter of Miguel, Duke of Braganza
- Prince Ludwig Philipp of Thurn and Taxis (2 February 1901 – 22 April 1933), married Princess Elisabeth of Luxembourg, daughter of Grand Duke William IV of Luxembourg
- Prince Max Emanuel of Thurn and Taxis (1 March 1902 – 3 October 1994)
- Princess Elisabeth Helene of Thurn and Taxis (15 December 1903 – 22 October 1976), married Friedrich Christian, Margrave of Meissen
- Prince Raphael Rainer of Thurn and Taxis (30 May 1906 – 8 June 1993), married Princess Margarete of Thurn and Taxis
- Prince Philipp Ernst of Thurn and Taxis (7 May 1908 – 23 July 1964), married Princess Eulalia of Thurn and Taxis

Titles and styles

- **6 July 1870 – 15 July 1890**: *Her Imperial and Royal Highness* Archduchess and Princess Margarethe Klementine of Austria; Princess Margarethe Klementine of Hungary, Bohemia, and Tuscany
- **15 July 1890 – 22 January 1952**: *Her Imperial and Royal Highness* The Princess of Thurn and Taxis
- **22 January 1952 – 2 May 1955**: *Her Imperial and Royal Highness* The Dowager Princess of Thurn and Taxis

Source (edited): "http://en.wikipedia.org/wiki/Archduchess_Margarethe_Klementine_of_Austria"

Baroness Wilhelmine of Dörnberg

Baroness *Wilhelmine* Caroline Christiane Henriette of Dörnberg, full German name: *Wilhelmine Caroline Christiane Henriette, Reichsfreiin von Dörnberg* (born 6 March 1803 in Ansbach, Kingdom of Prussia; died 14 May 1835 in Nuremberg, Kingdom of Bavaria) was a member of the House of Dörnberg and a Baroness of Dörnberg by birth. Through her marriage to Maximilian Karl, 6th Prince of Thurn and Taxis, Wilhelmine was also a member of the House of Thurn and Taxis. Wilhelmine was known to her family and friends as "Mimi."

Early life

Wilhelmine was the daughter of the former royal Prussian vice president and director of the chamber to the Ansbach domain, Baron Heinrich Ernst Konrad Friedrich of Dörnberg and his wife Baroness Sophie Wilhelmine of Glauburg.

Marriage and issue

Wilhelmine married Maximilian Karl, 6th Prince of Thurn and Taxis, fourth child of Karl Alexander, 5th Prince of Thurn and Taxis and his wife Duchess Therese of Mecklenburg-Strelitz, on 24 August 1828 in Regensburg. Wilhelmine and Maximilian Karl had five

children:
- Prince Karl Wilhelm of Thurn and Taxis (14 April 1829 – 21 July 1829)
- Princess Therese Mathilde of Thurn and Taxis (31 August 1830 – 10 September 1883)
- Maximilian Anton Lamoral, Hereditary Prince of Thurn and Taxis (28 September 1831 – 26 June 1867)
- Prince Egon of Thurn and Taxis (17 November 1832 – 8 February 1892)
- Prince Theodor of Thurn and Taxis (9 February 1834 – 1 March 1876)

Wilhelmine's family, the House of Dörnberg, was a Protestant Hessian noble family and was not, according to the laws of the Princely House of Thurn and Taxis House Act of 1776, not equal to her husband Maximilian Karl. Despite the fierce resistance to the union from the members of the princely house, especially from Maximilian Karl's mother Therese, the two married.

Illness and death

In 1834, Wilhelmine fell ill on a hard drive to the Thurn and Taxis possessions in Bohemia including Castle Chraustowitz. At the beginning of 1835, the she went to Nuremberg to receive a homeopathic treatment with Dr. Reuter. Wilhelmine was hopeful that the treatments would restore her quality of life. However, she died on 14 May 1835.

Titles and styles

- **6 March 1803 – 24 August 1828**: Baroness Wilhelmine of Dörnberg
- **24 August 1828 – 14 May 1835**: *Her Serene Highness* The Princess of Thurn and Taxis, Baroness of Dörnberg

Source (edited): "http://en.wikipedia.org/wiki/Baroness_Wilhelmine_of_D%C3%B6rnberg"

Carlo Alessandro, 3rd Duke of Castel Duino

Carlo Alessandro, Prince della Torre e Tasso, 3rd Duke of Castel Duino, full Italian name: *Carlo Alessandro, Principe della Torre e Tasso, Duca di Castel Duino* (born 10 February 1952 at Neuilly-sur-Seine, Île-de-France, France) is the current head of the Castel Duino branch of the House of Thurn and Taxis.

Family

Carlo Alessandro is the only child of Raimundo, 2nd Duke of Castel Duino and his wife Princess Eugénie of Greece and Denmark.

Marriage and issue

Carlo Alessandro married Veronique Lantz, daughter of Gérard Lantz and his wife Monique Rachet, on 10 February 1976 in Saint-Tropez, Provence-Alpes-Côte d'Azur, France. Carlo Alessandro and Veronique have three children:
- Prince Dimitri della Torre e Tasso (born 24 November 1977)
- Prince Maximilian della Torre e Tasso (born 22 May 1979)
- Princess Constanza della Torre e Tasso (born 7 August 1989)

Carlo Alessandro and his family currently reside at Duino Castle in the Province of Trieste, Italy.

Titles, styles, honours and arms

Titles and styles

- **10 February 1952 – 17 March 1986**: *His Serene Highness* Prince Carlo Alessandro della Torre e Tasso
- **17 March 1986 – present**: *His Serene Highness* The Duke of Castel Duino

Source (edited): "http://en.wikipedia.org/wiki/Carlo_Alessandro,_3rd_Duke_of_Castel_Duino"

Czech branch of the House of Thurn and Taxis

The **Czech branch of the Princely House of Thurn and Taxis** (German: *Das Fürstenhaus Thurn und Taxis*) is a dynastic branch of a German family that was a key player in the postal services in Europe in the 16th century and is well known as owners of breweries and builders of countless castles.

History

The Czech branch of the House of Thurn und Taxis was founded in 1808 by **Prince Maximilian Joseph von Thurn und Taxis** (Regensburg, 29 May 1769 – Prague, 15 May 1831). He was the youngest child of Alexander Ferdinand, 3rd Prince of Thurn and Taxis (1704 – 1773), a founder of a dynastic order of knighthood and a house order of chivalry in the Princely House of Thurn and Taxis, The Order of Parfaite Amitié, and his third wife Princess Maria Henriette von Fürstenberg (1732 – 1772). In 1791, Maximilian married Princess Eleonore von Lobkowicz (Prague, 22 April 1770 – Lautschin, 9 November 1834), who belonged to a mediatised Czech noble family whose origin can be traced back to Mares Martin z Ujezda (1376–90). In 1808, he inherited Lautschin (Loučeň in Czech) and Dobrovice castles from his cousin Princess Maria Josefa von Fürstenberg, and in 1820 permanently settled in Bohemia. Besides Lautschin and other rural estates, the family also owned real estate in Prague that included two palaces: one in the city's uptown (V jámě 635–636, no longer exists) and one in the old town (Vrtbovský Palace in Malá Strana, purchased in 1814). Maximilian and Eleonore had six sons: the firstborn was Karl Anselm von Thurn und Taxis (not to be confused with his uncle Karl Anselm, 4th Prince of Thurn and Taxis of Regensburg, heir to the House of Thurn und Taxis wealth).

In 1815 **Prince Karl Anselm von Thurn und Taxis** (Prague, 18 June 1792 – Teplitz, 25 August 1844) married Countess Marie Isabelle von und zu Eltz Faust von Stromberg (Dresden, 10 February 1795 – Prague, 12 March 1859). They had six children: Marie Sophie (Countess von Montfort), Hugo (heir to the family estate), Eleonore, Emerich, Marie Theresa (Countess von Belcredi), and Rudolf, who became Baron von Troskow.

Rudolf von Troskow

Rudolf, Baron von Troskow (Prague, 25 November 1833 – Velehrad, 4 July 1904) married morganatically in 1857 Jenny Ständler (Prague, 9 April 1830 – Graz, 28 September 1914). Rudolf was an intellectual who loved Czech music and literature and was an avid patron of the arts. He studied law and in 1861 founded "Právník," the first Czech language law journal. Aided by Karel Jaromír Erben, he also contributed vocabulary to Czech legal terminology.

He was sincerely devoted to the Czech national cause and was one of its important players: he was the publisher of "Boleslavan," a Czech language weekly dedicated to the cause, and became the first chairman of the famous Czech choir Hlahol. He was also a member of the Committee for the Establishment of the Czech National Theatre (1861) and one of the founders of Czech arts society Umělecká beseda in Prague (1863). He supported Czech writers Božena Němcová, Vítězslav Hálek, and Karolina Světlá, and promoted Czech composers Antonín Dvořák and Bedřich Smetana. The latter composed the opera *Braniboři v Čechách* at Rudolf's estate in Niměřice. In 1894, Rudolf gave up his princely title and family name, receiving at his request the title of *Freiherr von Troskow* from the Emperor Franz Joseph. Ten years later he died while visiting his daughter Hedvika in Velehrad. In 1930, his and his wife's remains were exhumed and reinterred in the family grave in Stará Boleslav.

Hugo Maximilian von Thurn und Taxis

Prince Hugo Maximilian von Thurn und Taxis (Prague, 3 July 1817 – Lautschin, 28 November 1889) married Countess Almeria von Belcredi (Ingrowitz, 8 October 1819 – Lautschin, 25 September 1914). Hugo's estate included castles in Dobrovice, Lautschin (Loucen in Czech) and Mzells (Mcely), and estates in Vlkava, Niměřice and Ceteň. Hugo had four legitimate children: Karoline, Egmont (who died young), Alexander (his heir), and Maria Theresia.

Alexander and Marie von Thurn und Taxis

Prince Alexander Johann Vincenz Rudolf Hugo Karl Lamoral Eligius von Thurn und Taxis (Lautschin, 1 December 1851 – Lautschin, 21 July 1939) married in 1875 Princess Marie zu Hohenlohe-Waldenburg-Schillingsfürst (Venice, 28 December 1855 – Lautschin, 16 February 1934). They inherited Lautschin in 1889. Both Alexander and Marie were avid patrons of the arts (Alexander himself played violin and Marie was an amateur painter), and although they were not wealthy compared to their Regensburg relatives, they were generous and never hesitated to support a good cause.

Marie's protégé Rainer Maria Rilke used to visit the family at their castles Lautschin and Duino. He dedicated his *Duino Elegies* to the princess, who in turn wrote about him in her published memoirs. Besides Rilke, regular guests at the castle in Lautschin included Karel Sladkovský and Bedřich Smetana who in 1880 dedicated his composition *Z domoviny* for violin and piano to Alexander. After Smetana's death, Alexander designated the house in nearby Jabkenice, where Smetana lived his last years, as Smetana's museum and donated land for his memorial. Other artists known to visit the castle included F. X. Šalda, Eliška Krásnohorská, Karel Bendl, members of the Czech Quartet (who included composer Josef Suk), and Mark Twain (who visited the castle during his European travels in 1899). Alexander also loved to travel and he was a passionate hunter who made several hunting trips to Africa, occasionally accompanied by Czech traveller Bedřich Machulka; he later donated his animal trophies to the National Museum in Prague. He belonged to the Knights of Malta and financially assisted a number of charitable causes. Together with his father Prince Hugo he was also instrumental in building the first railway in the region. The railway was built on land that he donated for the project.

When his son Prince Erich, who studied in Cambridge, brought to Lautschin a new game, he helped him establish the first football team in Bohemia (1889). The team made history when it played in the first official football match historically recorded in Bohemia (1893). The Lautschin team competed against Regatta, the best team in the Austrian-Hungarian Empire. The match took place at the famous Císařská louka in Prague on 18 April 1893 and ended with the Thurn Taxis team losing 0:5. This was still considered a great success for the Lautschin players and the Vienna newspapers Wiener Sportzeitung did not hesitate to conclude that the team from Lautschin was the second best team after Regatta in the Empire. The family's burial place is in Syčín (Seitzin) near Dobrovice.

Prince Alexander had three legitimate children: Erich (Mzells, 11 January 1876 – Kremsegg, 20 October 1952), Eugen (Prague, 27 March 1878 – Prague, 4 March 1903), and Alexander (Mzells, 8 July 1881 – Duino, 11 March 1937). Erich married Countess Gabrielle Kinsky (eldest daughter of Rudolf, 9th Prince Kinsky of Wchinitz and Tettau) in 1903 and in 1925 moved to Austria where he died in 1952. He had nine children, and his son Alexander Ferdinand (1906–1992) held the Lautschin Castle until the end of the war in 1945 when it was confiscated by the Czechoslovak state (his cousin, Ludwig (Luigi) held Mzells Castle until 1948).

Erich's brother Alexander moved to Italy in 1923 where he died at Duino Castle in 1937, having divorced his first wife, Princess Marie de Ligne in 1919, emigrated to Italy and left the dynastic House of Thurn und Taxis to become the first *Duca di Castel Duino* by grant of Victor Emmanuel III of Italy. His sons emigrated with their father and were recognized in Italy as *Principes della Torre e Tasso*, although Alexander's daughter Princess Margarita re-

mained a member of the Thurn und Taxis family until her marriage in 1931 to Prince Gaetano of Bourbon-Parma. After Alexander's death, the castle in Duino was inherited by his son Raimundo, 2nd Duke of Castel Duino (1907–1986), and has remained a part of the Torre e Tasso family estate. Descendants of the House of Thurn und Taxis in Bohemia, a family that played an important part in Czech national culture and local history for 140 years, are today dispersed around the world.
Source (edited): "http://en.wikipedia.org/wiki/Czech_branch_of_the_House_of_Thurn_and_Taxis"

Duchess Auguste of Württemberg

Duchess *Auguste* Elisabeth of Württemberg (in German: *Auguste Elisabeth, Herzogin von Württemberg*; 30 October 1734, Stuttgart, Duchy of Württemberg, Holy Roman Empire– 4 June 1787, Hornberg, Duchy of Württemberg, Holy Roman Empire) was a member of the Ducal House of Württemberg and a Duchess of Württemberg by birth. Through her marriage to Karl Anselm, 4th Prince of Thurn and Taxis, Auguste was also a member of the Princely House of Thurn and Taxis and Princess consort of Thurn and Taxis.

Family and early life

Auguste was the sixth and youngest child of Karl Alexander, Duke of Württemberg and his wife Princess Maria Augusta of Thurn and Taxis. In her youth, she had lived with her mother, until she entered the exclusive Ursuline convent in Metz in 1750. In 1752, her eldest brother Karl Eugen had wanted her to marry a French prince of the blood to assist in his reorientation of Württemberg policy towards France. The match fell through however, and to save the cost of maintaining Auguste, she was instead married off to her maternal cousin Karl Anselm, 4th Prince of Thurn and Taxis.

Marriage and issue

Auguste married Karl Anselm, 4th Prince of Thurn and Taxis, son of Alexander Ferdinand, 3rd Prince of Thurn and Taxis and his wife Margravine Sophie Christine of Brandenburg-Bayreuth, on 3 September 1753 in Stuttgart, Duchy of Württemberg. They had eight children:
- Princess Maria Theresia of Thurn and Taxis (born 10 July 1757 † 9 March 1776)
∞ 25 August 1774 Kraft Ernst, Prince of Oettingen-Oettingen
- Princess Sophie Friederike of Thurn and Taxis (born 20 July 1758; † 31 May 1800)
∞ 31 December 1775 Prince Hieronim Wincenty Radziwiłł (11 May 1759-18 September 1786)
∞ around 1795 NN Kazanowski
∞ 1797 to a Count Ostrorog
- Prince Franz Johann Nepomuck of Thurn and Taxis (baptized 2 October 1759; † 22 January 1760)
- Princess Henrica Karoline of Thurn and Taxis (baptized 25 April 1762; † 25 April 1784)
∞ 21 April 1783 with Johannes Aloysius II, Prince of Oettingen-Oettingen and Oettingen-Spielberg
- Prince Alexander Karl of Thurn and Taxis (born 19 April 1763; † 21 April 1763)
- Princess Friederike Dorothea of Thurn and Taxis (born 11 September 1764 † 10 November 1764)
- Karl Alexander, 5th Prince of Thurn and Taxis (born 22 February 1770; † 15 July 1827)
∞ 25 May 1789 with Duchess Therese of Mecklenburg-Strelitz
- Prince Friedrich Johann Nepomuck of Thurn and Taxis (born 11 April 1772 † 7 December 1805), unmarried

Titles, styles, honours and arms

Titles and styles

- **30 October 1734 – 3 September 1753**: *Her Ducal Serene Highness* Duchess Auguste of Württemberg
- **3 September 1753 – 17 March 1773**: *Her Ducal Serene Highness* The Hereditary Princess of Thurn and Taxis
- **17 March 1773–1776**: *Her Ducal Serene Highness* The Princess of Thurn and Taxis
- **1776 – 4 June 1787**: *Her Ducal Serene Highness* Princess Auguste of Thurn and Taxis, Duchess of Württemberg

Source (edited): "http://en.wikipedia.org/wiki/Duchess_Auguste_of_W%C3%BCrttemberg"

Duchess Helene in Bavaria

Helene Caroline Therese, Duchess in Bavaria (4 April 1834 in Munich, Bavaria - 16 May 1890 in Regensburg, Bavaria) of the House of Wittelsbach, nicknamed Néné, was a Bavarian princess and, through marriage, temporarily the head of the Thurn and Taxis family.

Family

Helene was the oldest daughter of Maximilian Joseph, Duke in Bavaria and Ludovika, Royal Princess of Bavaria. The family home was at Possenhofen Castle.

Marriage

In 1853 she traveled with her mother Ludovika and her younger sister Elisabeth to the resort of Bad Ischl, Upper Austria with the hopes that she would become the bride of their cousin Franz Josef, then the emperor of Austria. He decided that he preferred Elisabeth instead. Helene was unusually pious, and would have fit into the Habsburg court well. She had one quality, though, that would not have been accepted: she was habitually late, and often missed trains and appointments.

Helene's husband Maximilian

After the failed engagement, she became depressed and Ludovika became concerned that Helene would take the veil and join a convent. Helene had almost come to terms with remaining single. At 22 years old she was considered to be an "old maid," but her mother arranged for her to meet the wealthy Maximilian Anton Lamoral, Hereditary Prince of Thurn and Taxis. Duke Max in Bavaria, Helene's father, invited the Thurn and Taxis family to Possenhofen for a hunting party, at which Prince Maximilian was introduced to Helene.

While the prince was vacationing at Possenhofen, he brought his marriage plans to his parents, who immediately agreed. The only difficulty involved was that although the Thurn and Taxis family were counted among the richest in the land, they were not considered social equals for a princess of royal blood and a member of the House of Wittelsbach. Because of this, King Maximilian II of Bavaria did not at first agree to a marriage between the two, but through Elisabeth's influence on the king, the marriage took place nevertheless. The wedding ceremony was held on 24 August 1858 at Possenhofen. To mark the occasion, the in-laws gave the bride a necklace worth 160,000 Gulden. Ironically, in spite of the earlier objections to the match, Helene is considered to have had the only happy marriage among the five Wittelsbach sisters.

Her daughter Louisa was born in 1859, followed by a second daughter, Elisabeth, in 1860. Shortly after the birth of her second child she traveled to Corfu to visit her sister Elisabeth, who was very ill. She returned by way of Vienna, where she reported to Franz Josef on the poor state of his wife.

She gave birth to the much-desired son in 1862, named Maximilian Maria, and in 1867 had another son named Albert.

Even though the couple had a happy marriage, it was overshadowed by the severe illness of her husband Maximilian, who had chronic kidney disease. Neither a course of treatment in Karlsbad nor the best doctors could save him. He died in 1867 at only 36 years of age.

Later life

Helene took her mind off her sorrows with charitable activities. She received the guardianship of her children from the Austrian emperor. Her father-in-law began to include her in the business affairs of the House of Thurn and Taxis, seeing in her a support and successor. In this way she became the head of the family until her oldest son reached his majority.

In 1877 her youngest daughter Elisabeth married Prince Miguel of Braganza, the Miguelist claimant to the throne of Portugal. Elisabeth's health deteriorated after the birth of her first child, and she eventually died in 1881.

In 1879 Helene's oldest daughter Louise married the young Prince Frederick of Hohenzollern-Sigmaringen. The couple had no children.

In 1883, her son Maximilian took over the leadership of the family business, but the well-trained young man fell ill. His heart had been weakened by scarlet fever in childhood, and he suffered from severe heart spasms. In 1885, he died of a pulmonary embolism. This left Helene the family head again, until 1888 when her son Albert reached his majority and took over the family businesses. Helene then retired and dedicated herself to her religious devotions.

She became very ill with stomach cancer in 1890, and her sister Elisabeth hurried to her side. Elisabeth was the last person to speak with Helene. Elisabeth's daughter Marie Valerie related in her diary, "Aunt Néné ... was glad to see Mama and said to her, 'Old Sisi' -- she and Mama almost always spoke English together. 'We two have had hard puffs in our lives,' said Mama. 'Yes, but we had hearts,' replied Aunt Néné."

Titles and styles

- 4 April 1834 – 24 August 1858 *Her Royal Highness* Duchess Helene in Bavaria
- 24 August 1858 – 16 May 1890 *Her Royal Highness* the Hereditary Princess of Thurn and Taxis

Source (edited): "http://en.wikipedia.org/wiki/Duchess_Helene_in_Bavaria"

Duchess Therese of Mecklenburg-Strelitz

Duchess Therese Mathilde Amalie of Mecklenburg-Strelitz (German: *Herzogin Therese Mathilde Amalie zu Mecklenburg-Strelitz*; 5 April 1773 – 12 February 1839) was a member of the House of Mecklenburg-Strelitz and a Duchess of Mecklenburg. Through her marriage to Karl Alexander, 5th Prince of Thurn and Taxis, Therese was also a member of the House of Thurn and Taxis.

Family

Therese Mathilde Amalie of Mecklenburg was born in Hanover the daughter of Duke Charles of Mecklenburg and his first wife Princess Friederike of Hesse-Darmstadt.

Therese married Karl Alexander, Hereditary Prince of Thurn and Taxis, son of Karl Anselm, 4th Prince of Thurn and Taxis and his wife Duchess Auguste of Württemberg, on 25 May 1789 in Neustrelitz, Mecklenburg-Strelitz. Therese and Karl Alexander had seven children:
- Princess Charlotte Luise of Thurn and Taxis (24 March 1790 – 22 October 1790)
- Prince George Karl of Thurn and Taxis (26 March 1792 – 20 January 1795)
- Princess Maria Theresia of Thurn and Taxis (6 July 1794 – 18 August 1874)
- Princess Luise Friederike of Thurn and Taxis (29 August 1798 – 1 December 1798)
- Princess Maria Sophia Dorothea of Thurn and Taxis (4 March 1800 – 20 December 1870)
- Maximilian Karl, 6th Prince of Thurn and Taxis (3 November 1802 – 10 November 1871)
- Prince Friedrich Wilhelm of Thurn and Taxis (29 January 1805 – 7 September 1825)

Therese also had illegitimate issue by Maximilian, Graf von und zu Lerchenfeld auf Köfering und Schönberg (München, 17 January 1772 – Kassel, 19 October 1809), who married on 25 May 1789 Maria Anna Philippine Walburga Groschlag von Dieburg, by whom he had one son; one was created Graf von Stockau; the others were surnamed von Stargard. Children include:
- Georg Adolf, Graf von Stockau (Dresden, Saxony, 6 May 1806 – Napajedl castle, Maehren, 4 April 1865, bur. crypt, Napajedl castle chapel, Maehren), a Lutheran, married on 25 November 1830 to Franziska de Paula Maria Elisabeth, Gräfin von Fünfkirchen (Vienna, Austria, 24 July 1801 – Napajedl castle, Maehren, 14 May 1870, bur. crypt, Napajedl castle chapel, Maehren), a Roman Catholic, heiress of Napajedl castle and estate in Maehren, widow of Clemens Graf von Kesselstatt, and had issue, now seemingly extinct in male line
- Amalie von Sternfeld (Regensburg, 16 June 1808 – Tegernsee, 21 June 1888), married at Köfering, 31 August 1825 to Georg-Alexander, Freiherr von Krüdener (1786 – 1852), and had female issue

After the mediatization of the Principality of Thurn and Taxis to the Kingdom of Bavaria in 1806 during the German Mediatisations, the end of the Holy Roman Empire and creation of the Confederation of the Rhine, and the subsequent end of the Imperial Reichspost, Therese's initiative and negotiating skills were influential in maintaining the Thurn and Taxis-run postal system as the private company, Thurn-und-Taxis-Post. Like her sister, Louise, Queen consort of Prussia, she failed in their negotiations with Napoleon I of France, but during the Congress of Vienna, she was successful in enforcing the interests of the Thurn and Taxis family.

Political activities

Therese and Karl Alexander had their first residence (until 1797) in the Palais Thurn und Taxis in Frankfurt am Main. Early on in their marriage, Therese took over her young husband's representational tasks. After her father-in-law's resignation as Post Master General and Principal Commissioner of the Perpetual Imperial Diet at Regensburg, Therese's husband Karl Alexander became Principal Commissioner in 1797. Therese took an active role in the administration of the Princely House and lands as well as the postal administration and was also devoted to art and literature. She hosted in her salon poets and writers including Jean Paul, Friedrich Rückert, Johann Kaspar Lavater, and Friedrich Gottlieb Klopstock.

The Hereditary Princess of Thurn and Taxis, oil on canvas by Carlo Restallino, Regensburg in 1800.

Only with the predictable demise of the Imperial Reichspost, the German Mediatisations of 1803, the mediatization of the Princely House of Thurn and Taxis, and the loss of position of Post Master General in the time of Napoleon I of France, Therese became outwardly politically active, most especially after the death of her father-in-law in 1805. Since then, Therese reinforced the sovereignty of the Princely House of Thurn and Taxis and its traditional postal rights. In 1806, she and her husband negotiated with her brother-in-law Frederick William III of Prussia along with Karl Theodor Anton Maria von Dalberg, the former Archbishop-Elector of Mainz and Prince-Primate of Regensburg, and for the first time in 1807 with Napoleon. Likewise, they also negotiated with Maximilian I Joseph of Bavaria in Munich and proposed to him the nationalization of the Thurn and Taxis Lehnspost there. In 1808, Therese and her husband took the interests of the Princely House of Thurn and Taxis to the Congress of Erfurt. There, a secret meeting occurred between Charles Maurice de Talleyrand-Périgord and Alexander I of Russia in her salon.

After fruitless negotiations in Erfurt

were lost, Therese traveled at the end of 1809 to Paris, where she met with Napoleon concerning the future status of the Princely House of Thurn and Taxis, the withdrawal of the media, and the re-acquisition of rights to the postal system. From this trip survives a correspondence with her husband Karl Alexander in which he laments the impoverishment of the House of Thurn and Taxis and asks Therese to limit her expenses. Through their negotiations with Napoleon, the Princely House of Thurn and Taxis was offered to relocate to Paris. The negotiations failed, however, perhaps because the correspondence with her sister Queen Louise of Prussia fell into the hands of the French authorities.

After the defeat and exile of Napoleon, Therese took the interests of the Princely House to the Congress of Vienna in 1814 where many political negotiations took place between Talleyrand, Tsar Alexander I, Klemens Wenzel, Prince von Metternich, and other political leaders in her salon. Not least because of Article 17 of the Federal Act from the year 1815, the revenue of the former post offices of the House of Thurn and Taxis in several states of the German Confederation as a legitimate claim was established. Private postal services were established and were intended to have a reasonable compensation obligation to the Princely House of Thurn and Taxis.

Duchess Therese died in Taxis, Regensburg, at the age of 65.

Titles and styles
- **5 April 1773 – 25 May 1789**: *Her Serene Highness* Duchess Therese of Mecklenburg-Strelitz
- **25 May 1789 – 13 November 1805**: *Her Serene Highness* The Heredtiary Princess of Thurn and Taxis
- **13 November 1805 – 28 June 1815**: *Her Serene Highness* The Princess of Thurn and Taxis
- **28 June 1815 – 15 July 1827**: *Her Highness* The Princess of Thurn and Taxis
- **15 July 1827 – 12 February 1839**: *Her Highness* The Dowager Princess of Thurn and Taxis

Source (edited): "http://en.wikipedia.org/wiki/Duchess_Therese_of_Mecklenburg-Strelitz"

Duke of Castel Duino

The **Dukes of Castel Duino** are a noble family in Italy descending from the Bohemian line of the Princely House of Thurn and Taxis. The title was created along with the additional title of **Prince della Torre e Tasso** in 1923 for Prince Alexander of Thurn and Taxis following his naturalisation in Kingdom of Italy. The second duke, Raimundo, married Princess Eugénie of Greece and Denmark a member of the Greek Royal Family.

The seat of the family is Duino Castle in Duino in the Province of Trieste, Friuli-Venezia Giulia.

Dukes of Castel Duino (1923-present)

- Prince Alessandro della Torre e Tasso, 1st Duke of Castel Duino (1881-1937), son of Prince Alexander Johann of Thurn and Taxis and Princess Marie of Hohenlohe-Waldenburg-Schillingsfürst
- Prince Raimundo della Torre e Tasso, 2nd Duke of Castel Duino (1907-1986)
- Prince Carlo Alessandro della Torre e Tasso, 3rd Duke of Castel Duino (born 1952)

The heir is Prince Dimitri della Torre e Tasso (born 1977).

Source (edited): "http://en.wikipedia.org/wiki/Duke_of_Castel_Duino"

Eugen Alexander Franz, 1st Prince of Thurn and Taxis

Eugen Alexander Franz, **Prince of Thurn and Taxis**, full German name: *Eugen Alexander Franz Fürst von Thurn und Taxis* (baptized 11 January 1652 in Brussels, Spanish Netherlands; died 21 February 1714 in Frankfurt am Main, Free Imperial City of Frankfurt, Holy Roman Empire) was the first Prince of Thurn and Taxis, Postmaster General of the Imperial Reichspost, and Head of the House of Thurn and Taxis from 13 September 1676 until his death.

Early life

Eugen Alexander Franz was the second son of Lamoral II Claudius Franz, Count of Thurn and Taxis and his wife Countess Anna Franziska Eugenia of Horn. The date of his birth is unknown, but Eugen Alexander Franz was baptised on 11 January 1652 in Brussels.

Postmaster General

After the death of his father, Eugen Alexander Franz succeeded to the positions of Postmaster General of the Imperial Reichspost and the Spanish Netherlands. In 1681, the last Habsburg King of Spain Charles II appointed Eugen Alexander Franz from a count to a prince, and Leopold I, Holy Roman Emperor made him an Imperial prince in 1695.

After the French occupation of the Spanish Netherlands during the War of the Spanish Succession, the new Spanish King Philip V, grandson of Louis XIV of France, deposed Eugen Alexander Franz as Post Master General of the Spanish Netherlands. In 1702, he moved his postal system's headquarters from Brussels to Frankfurt am Main where it originated.

Marriage and issue

Eugen Alexander Franz was married twice. He married first to Princess Anna Adelheid of Fürstenberg-Heiligenberg, youngest daughter and child of Hermann Egon, Count of Fürstenberg-Heiligenberg and his wife Countess Franziska of Fürstenberg-Stühlingen. Eugen Alexander Franz and Anna Adelheid had the following children:

- Countess Dorothea of Thurn and Taxis (born and died in 1679)
- a son whose name is unknown (born and died in 1680)
- Anselm Franz, 2nd Prince of Thurn and Taxis (1681-1739) married Maria Ludovika Anna Franziska, Princess of Lobkowicz
- Count Jakob Lamoral of Thurn and Taxis (?-?)
- Count Heinrich Franz of Thurn and Taxis (born and died in 1682)
- Countess Anna Franziska of Thurn and Taxis (born and died in 1683)
- Countess Eleonora Ferdinanda of Thurn and Taxis (born and died in 1685)
- Count Inigo Lamoral Maria Felix Franz of Thurn and Taxis (born and died in 1686)
- Countess Anna Theresia of Thurn and Taxis (born and died in 1689)
- Countess Maria Elisabeth of Thurn and Taxis (born and died in 1691)

After the death of his first wife, Eugen Alexander Franz married Countess Anna Augusta of Hohenlohe-Waldenburg-Schillingsfürst, daughter of Ludwig Gustav, Count of Hohenlohe-Waldenburg-Schillingsfürst and his second wife Anna Barbara von Schönborn. Eugen Alexander Franz and Anna Augusta had the following children:

- Prince Lothar Franz of Thurn and Taxis (1705-1712)
- Prince Maximilian Philipp of Thurn and Taxis (born and died in 1706)
- Prince Philipp Lamoral of Thurn and Taxis (born and died in 1708)
- Princess Maria Josepha of Thurn and Taxis (born and died in 1711)

Titles, styles, honours and arms

Titles and styles

- **11 January 1652 – 13 September 1676**: *His Serene Highness* The Hereditary Count of Thurn and Taxis
- **13 September 1676 – 1695**: *His Serene Highness* The Count of Thurn and Taxis
- **1695 – 21 February 1714**: *His Serene Highness* The Prince of Thurn and Taxis

Honours

- Knight of the Austrian Order of the Golden Fleece

Source (edited): "http://en.wikipedia.org/wiki/Eugen_Alexander_Franz,_1st_Prince_of_Thurn_and_Taxis"

Franz Joseph, 9th Prince of Thurn and Taxis

Franz Joseph **Maximilian Maria Antonius Ignatius Lamoral, Prince of Thurn and Taxis**, full German name: *Franz Josef Maximilian Maria Antonius Ignatius Lamoral Fürst von Thurn und Taxis* (born 21 December 1893 in Regensburg, Kingdom of Bavaria; died 13 July 1971 in Regensburg, Bavaria, Germany) was the ninth Prince of Thurn and Taxis and Head of the Princely House of Thurn and Taxis from 22 January 1952 until his death on 13 July 1971.

Early life

Franz Joseph was the eldest son of Albert, 8th Prince of Thurn and Taxis and his wife Archduchess Margarethe Klementine of Austria.

His christening was attended by Franz Joseph I of Austria. Franz Joseph had six younger brothers and a sister. One of his brothers was Prince Max Emanuel of Thurn and Taxis (1902–1994), a member of the Order of Saint Benedict known as Pater Emmeram.

Education and World War I service

Franz Joseph received a humanistic education by private teachers. Beginning in the winter semester of 1912, Franz Joseph studied at both the University of Strasbourg and University of Leipzig. Because of the outbreak of World War I, he could not complete his studies. On 6 August 1914, Franz Joseph joined the Prussian Elite Regiment Garde de Corps.

During the war, he was promoted to lieutenant. After the war's end in January 1919, Franz Joseph returned to Regensburg.

Marriage and family

Franz Joseph married Princess Isabel Maria of Braganza, daughter of Miguel, Duke of Braganza and his wife Princess Maria Theresa of Löwenstein-Wertheim-Rosenberg, on 23 November 1920 at Schloss Bronnbach, Bronnbach, Wertheim, Bavaria, Germany.

Franz Joseph and Isabel Maria had five children:

- Prince Gabriel of Thurn and Taxis (16 October 1922 – 17 December 1942)
- Prince Michaele of Thurn and Taxis (16 October 1922 – 17 October 1922)
- Princess Helene of Thurn and Taxis (27 May 1924 – 27 October 1991)
- Princess Maria Theresia of Thurn and Taxis (10 September 1925 – 27 April 1997)
- Princess Maria Ferdinande of Thurn and Taxis (born 19 December 1927)

Together with his wife, Franz Joseph resided at Schloss Haus in Neueglofsheim (Upper Palatinate) where he managed the property and its interests. There, he also took an interest in hunting, history, and art then. He later bequeathed Schloss Haus's large private library to the Prince Thurn und Taxis Hofbibliothek.

At the age of 46, Franz Joseph served Nazi Germany in the Invasion of Poland in 1939. By the end of June 1940, he was serving in the Battle of France. Subsequently, Franz Joseph was a crew chief stationed in France for two and a half years until he was dismissed due to a decree from Adolf Hitler on the "inability of the German Defense nobility" retroactive to 31 March 1944 by Generalfeldmarschall Wilhelm Keitel of the Army.

Franz Joseph's son Gabriel was killed in action on 17 December 1942 in the Battle of Stalingrad.

Franz Joseph resided for most of the year at Schloss Haus, but spent winters at Schloss Thurn und Taxis in Regensburg. In addition to managing the family estate, he dedicated himself increasingly to the preservation of the history of Regensburg and the former St. Emmeram's Abbey, the residence of the Princely House of Thurn and Taxis.

On 21 December 1963, Franz Joseph was made an Honorary Citizen of the City of Regensburg "in appreciation of the high contribution to the economic, social and cultural issues." He was also made an honorary member of the Roman Catholic student association K.D.St.V. Rupertia Regensburg.

Franz Joseph survived his wife Isabel Maria, who died on 12 January 1970, about one and a half years before him. He died after a severe illness on 13 July 1971 and was interred in the burial chapel at St. Emmeram's Abbey.

In Regensburg, the Erbprinz-Franz-Joseph-Straße is named after him.

Titles, styles, honours and arms

Titles and styles

- **21 December 1893 – 22 January 1952**: *His Serene Highness* The Hereditary Prince of Thurn and Taxis
- **22 January 1952 – 13 July 1971**: *His Serene Highness* The Prince of Thurn and Taxis

Honours

- Grand Cross with Star and Sash of the Order of Merit of the Federal Republic of Germany
- Grand Master of the Order of Parfaite Amitié

Source (edited): "http://en.wikipedia.org/wiki/Franz_Joseph,_9th_Prince_of_Thurn_and_Taxis"

Fritz von Thurn und Taxis

Fritz von Thurn und Taxis (born **Prince *Friedrich* Leonhard Ignatius Josef Maria Lamoral Balthasar of Thurn and Taxis** [full German name: *Friedrich Leonhard Ignatius Josef Maria Lamoral Balthasar, Prinz von Thurn und Taxis*] on 22 June 1950 in Linz, Upper Austria, Allied-occupied Austria) is an Austrian journalist and a member of the Bohemian line of the Princely House of Thurn and Taxis. He became well-known as a longtime sportscaster on the Bayerisches Fernsehen television channel. Since 1993, Thurn und Taxis has been a football commentator on the pay television channel Sky Deutschland.

Thurn und Taxis was the third child and second son of Prince Johann von Nepomuk of Thurn and Taxis and his wife Princess Maria Julia of Lobkowicz.

Career

His journalistic career began in 1971 with the Bayerischen Rundfunk. There, Thurn und Taxis worked in both television and in radio programs as a sports reporter and commentator and reported on several Olympic Games, football, skiing, and Ice Hockey World Championships events.

In honor of his years of reporting on the Ice Hockey World Championships, the International Ice Hockey Federation (IIHF) awarded Thurn und Taxis with an IIHF gold medal. Later, he hosted the sports magazine show *Blickpunkt Sport* on Bayerischen Rundfunk and moderated the *Sportschau* on ARD. Beginning in August 1993, Thurn und Taxis began hosting live Fußball-Bundesliga matches on the Munich-based pay television channel Sky Deutschland.

Thurn und Taxis married morganatically to Beata Béry, daughter of Laszlo Béry and his wife Countess Paula Apponyi de Nagy-Appony, on 4 June 1977 in Munich, Bavaria, Germany.

Titles, styles, honours and arms

Titles and styles

- **22 June 1950 – present**: *His Serene Highness* Prince Friedrich of Thurn and Taxis

Honours

- Knight of the Order of Parfaite Amitié

Source (edited): "http://en.wikipedia.org/wiki/Fritz_von_Thurn_und_Taxis"

Gloria, Princess of Thurn and Taxis

Gloria, Princess of Thurn and Taxis (born *Countess Mariae Gloria Ferdinanda Gerda Charlotte Teutonia Franziska Magarethe Frederike Simone Johanna Joachima Josefine Wilhelmine Huberta of Schönburg in Glauchau and Waldenburg*) is a princess, by marriage, of the German Thurn und Taxis House.

Biography

Gloria was born on 23 February 1960, the daughter of Joachim, Count of Schönburg-Glauchau and of Beatrix, Countess Széchenyi de Sárvár-Felsővidék. Her brother, Alexander, Count of Schönburg-Glauchau, is a best selling writer and journalist.

Although she was a countess, her family had little money, and she had worked as a waitress in the *chic* Swiss ski resort, St Moritz, before marrying Prince Johannes von Thurn und Taxis, who was born in 1926.

Known as the punk princess and "Princess TNT", Gloria was an icon in the 1980s. She was known for her exuberant and lavish spending and whirlwind social life. However, on Johannes's death, the spending came to a halt as massive taxes were due on the estate he left behind.

The couple had three children:
- Princess *Maria Theresia* Ludovika Klothilde Helene Alexandra of Thurn and Taxis, born 28 November 1980 in Regensburg
- Princess *Elisabeth* Margarethe Maria Anna Beatriz of Thurn and Taxis, born 24 March 1982 in Regensburg.
- Prince *Albert* Maria Lamoral Miguel Johannes Gabriel of Thurn and Taxis, born 24 June 1983 in Regensburg, who succeeded his father in 1990 as Albert II, Prince of Thurn and Taxis.

After her husband's death, Princess Gloria acted as a trustee for her underage son, Albert II, the new head of the House of Thurn und Taxis. During the trusteeship, Gloria controlled the $2 billion Thurn und Taxis fortune.

In 2001, she was severely criticized for stating in a talkshow that the high AIDS-rate in African countries was due not to a lack of safe sex practices but to the fact that "the blacks like to copulate ('schnackseln') a lot". In 2008, she said in an interview that the reason for the *higher copulate of blacks* is the higher heat in Africa.

Although the German Federal government does not recognize "noble" or "royal" status per se, members of the former royal, princely, and noble houses of German descent use their "titles" which the German government regards as last names. As a courtesy and for ease of use, female members of these families use the feminized version of the family name.

Titles
- **23 February 1960 - 31 May 1980** *Her Illustrious Highness* Countess Gloria of Schönburg-Glauchau
- **31 May 1980 - 26 April 1982** *Her Serene Highness* The Hereditary Princess of Thurn and Taxis
- **26 April 1982 - 14 December 1990** *Her Serene Highness* The Princess of Thurn and Taxis
- **14 December 1990 - present** *Her Serene Highness* The Dowager Princess of Thurn and Taxis

Source (edited): "http://en.wikipedia.org/wiki/Gloria_Princess_of_Thurn_and_Taxis"

House of Thurn and Taxis line of succession

The House of Thurn and Taxis exists through several extant lines descending from Alexander Ferdinand, 3rd Prince of Thurn and Taxis. The Law of Succession is agnatic primogeniture, only allowing males to succeed to the princely title. The current Head of the House of Thurn and Taxis is Albert, 12th Prince of Thurn and Taxis, styled as *His Serene Highness* The Prince of Thurn and Taxis.

- **Current prince**: HSH Albert, 12th Prince of Thurn and Taxis (born 1983)

Alexander Ferdinand → Karl Anselm → Karl Alexander → Maximilian Karl → Prince Maximilian Anton Lamoral → Albert I → Prince Raphael Rainer
- HSH Prince Max Emanuel of Thurn and Taxis (b. 1935), son of Prince Raphael Rainer of Thurn and Taxis

Alexander Ferdinand → Karl Anselm → Karl Alexander → Maximilian Karl → Prince Maximilian Anton Lamoral → Albert I → Prince Philipp Ernst
- HSH Prince Albrecht of Thurn and Taxis (b. 1930), son of Prince Philipp Ernst of Thurn and Taxis

Alexander Ferdinand → Prince Maximilian Joseph → Prince Karl Anselm → Prince Hugo Maximilian → Prince Alexander Johann → Prince Erich Lamoral → Prince Johann
- HSH Prince Friedrich of Thurn and Taxis (b. 1950), son of Prince Johann of Thurn and Taxis
- HSH Prince Karl Ferdinand of Thurn and Taxis (b. 1952), son of Prince Johann of Thurn and Taxis
- HSH Prince Maximilian of Thurn and Taxis (b. 1955), son of Prince Johann of Thurn and Taxis

Source (edited): "http://en.wikipedia.org/wiki/House_of_Thurn_and_Taxis_line_of_succession"

Johannes, 11th Prince of Thurn and Taxis

Johannes, Prince of Thurn and Taxis (5 June 1926 – 14 December 1990) was a German businessman and the head of the immensely wealthy, aristocratic Thurn und Taxis family from 1982 until his death.

Early life
Johannes was born in Regensburg, Germany, to Karl August, 10th Prince of Thurn and Taxis, and Princess Maria Anna of Braganza. He had two older sisters and one younger brother.

Marriage and family
The Thurn and Taxis family came to massive media attention during the late-1970s through mid-1980s when Johannes married the younger Countess Mariae Gloria of Schönburg-Glauchau, a member of an impoverished but mediatised noble family. The couple's wild, jet set lifestyle and Princess Gloria's over-the-top appearance (characterized by bright hair color and flashy clothes) earned her the nickname Princess TNT (also referred to as "Princess TNT, the dynamite socialite" according to the June 2006 edition of Vanity Fair Magazine). In the 1970s Johannes threw jet-set parties and, bisexual, was often seen in gay discos.

On 31 May 1980 Johannes, Prince

of Thurn and Taxis, married Gloria of Schönburg-Glauchau. They had three children:
- *Maria Theresia Ludowika Klothilde Helene Alexandra* (* 28 November 1980 in Regensburg),
- *Elisabeth Margarethe Maria Anna Beatriz* (* 24 March 1982 in Regensburg),
- *Albert (II.) Maria Lamoral Miguel Johannes Gabriel* (* 24 June 1983 in Regensburg).

From 1982, after the death of his father, Johannes became the head of the Thurn and Taxis family. On 14 December 1990 he died in Munich-Großhadern.

Honors
- Grand Master of the Order of Parfaite Amitié
- Bundesverdienstkreuz, 1985

Source (edited): "http://en.wikipedia.org/wiki/Johannes,_11th_Prince_of_Thurn_and_Taxis"

Karl Alexander, 5th Prince of Thurn and Taxis

Karl Alexander of Thurn and Taxis, full German name: *Karl Alexander Fürst von Thurn und Taxis* (born 22 February 1770 in the Imperial City of Regensburg, Holy Roman Empire; died 15 July 1827 at Schloss Taxis in Dischingen, Kingdom of Württemberg) was the fifth Prince of Thurn and Taxis, head of the Thurn-und-Taxis-Post, and Head of the Princely House of Thurn and Taxis from 13 November 1805 until his death on 15 July 1827. With the death of his father on 13 November 1805, he became nominal *Generalpostmeister* of the Imperial Reichspost until the resignation of Francis II, Holy Roman Emperor.

Early life

Karl Alexander studied at the Universities of Strasbourg, Würzburg, and Mainz and then subsequently went on a European tour. In 1797, he was appointed successor to his ailing father's position as *Prinzipalkommissar* at the *Immerwährender Reichstag* (German: *Perpetual Imperial Diet*) in Regensburg. Karl Alexander also worked for the Thurn and Taxis postal empire, operating during a decline due to the gradual loss of territory as a result of the Napoleonic Wars.

Marriage and family

Karl Alexander married Duchess Therese of Mecklenburg-Strelitz, fourth eldest child and third eldest daughter of Charles II, Grand Duke of Mecklenburg and his wife Princess Friederike of Hesse-Darmstadt, on 25 May 1789 in Neustrelitz, Mecklenburg-Strelitz. Karl Alexander and Therese had seven children:
- Princess Charlotte Luise of Thurn and Taxis (24 March 1790 – 22 October 1790)
- Prince George Karl of Thurn and Taxis (26 March 1792 – 20 January 1795)
- Princess Maria Theresia of Thurn and Taxis (6 July 1794 – 18 August 1874)
- Princess Luise Friederike of Thurn and Taxis (29 August 1798 – 1 December 1798)
- Princess Maria Sophia Dorothea of Thurn and Taxis (4 March 1800 – 20 December 1870)
- Maximilian Karl, 6th Prince of Thurn and Taxis (3 November 1802 – 10 November 1871)
- Prince Friedrich Wilhelm of Thurn and Taxis (29 January 1805 – 7 September 1825)

Continuation of the post

Karl Alexander, 5th Prince of Thurn and Taxis

After the end of the Holy Roman Empire, the Thurn and Taxis postal system continued to survive as a private company. Since 1806, Karl Alexander headed a private postal company, the Thurn-und-Taxis-Post. It existed first as a feud of some of the Confederation of the Rhine members, such as Baden, Bavaria, and Württemberg. Bavaria, however, nationalized the postal system two years later. After the Congress of Vienna, Karl Alexander took over the Hessian and Thuringian postal services, as well as those in the Hanseatic League cities of Bremen, Hamburg, and Lübeck, and Schaffhausen. From 1820, the company began to prosper again, so Karl Alexander began to acquire large amounts of land holdings.

Acquisition of new land

According to the Confederation of the Rhine Act, agreed upon between Napoleon I of France and the Confederation of the Rhine princes, the Principality of Thurn and Taxis lost its independence and was mediatised in 1806. Since then, the Princes of Thurn and Taxis and hence Karl Alexander, depending on the territory, were subjects of either the King of Württemberg, or the Princes of Hohenzollern-Sigmaringen. In return, the House of Thurn and Taxis received the Imperial Abbey of St. Emmeram and associated territories in Regensburg. Karl Alexander also received as the family head of the House of Thurn and Taxis, Prussian possessions in the Grand Duchy of Poland. In 1822/23, he bought from the Count Kinsky and others the Burg Richenburg in Bohemia.

Titles and styles
- **22 February 1770 – 17 March 1773**: *His Serene Highness* Prince Karl Alexander of Thurn and Taxis
- **17 March 1773 – 13 November 1805**: *His Serene Highness* The Hereditary Prince of Thurn and Taxis
- **13 November 1805 – 15 July 1827**: *His Serene Highness* The Prince of Thurn and Taxis

Honours
- Grand Master of the Order of Parfaite Amitié
- Knight of the Austrian Order of the Golden Fleece

Source (edited): "http://en.wikipedia.org/wiki/Karl_Alexander,_5th_Prince_of_Thurn_and_Taxis"

Karl Anselm, 4th Prince of Thurn and Taxis

Karl Anselm of Thurn and Taxis, full German name: *Karl Anselm Fürst von Thurn und Taxis* (born 2 June 1733 in Frankfurt am Main, Free Imperial City of Frankfurt, Holy Roman Empire; died 13 November 1805 in Winzer bei Regensburg, Electorate of Bavaria, Holy Roman Empire) was the fourth Prince of Thurn and Taxis, Postmaster General of the Imperial Reichspost, and Head of the Princely House of Thurn and Taxis from 17 March 1773 until his death on 13 November 1805. Karl Anselm served as *Prinzipalkommissar* at the *Immerwährender Reichstag* (German: *Perpetual Imperial Diet*) in Regensburg for Joseph II, Holy Roman Emperor and Francis II, Holy Roman Emperor from 1773 to 1797.

Early life

Karl Anselm was the eldest son of Alexander Ferdinand, 3rd Prince of Thurn and Taxis and his first wife Margravine Sophie Christine of Brandenburg-Bayreuth.

Marriages and family

Karl Anselm married Duchess Auguste of Württemberg, sixth and youngest child of Karl Alexander, Duke of Württemberg and his wife Princess Maria Augusta of Thurn and Taxis, on 3 September 1753 in Stuttgart, Duchy of Württemberg. Karl Anselm and Auguste had eight children:
- Princess Maria Theresia of Thurn and Taxis (born 10 July 1757 † 9 March 1776)
- ∞ 25 August 1774 Kraft Ernst, Prince of Oettingen-Oettingen
- Princess Sophie Friederike of Thurn and Taxis (born 20 July 1758; † 31 May 1800)
- ∞ 31 December 1775 Prince Hieronim Wincenty Radziwiłł (11 May 1759-18 September 1786)
- ∞ around 1795 NN Kazanowski
- ∞ 1797 to a Count Ostrorog
- Prince Franz Johann Nepomuck of Thurn and Taxis (baptized 2 October 1759; † 22 January 1760)
- Princess Henrica Karoline of Thurn and Taxis (baptized 25 April 1762; † 25 April 1784)
- ∞ 21 April 1783 with Johannes Aloysius II, Prince of Oettingen-Oettingen and Oettingen-Spielberg
- Prince Alexander Karl of Thurn and Taxis (born 19 April 1763; † 21 April 1763)
- Princess Friederike Dorothea of Thurn and Taxis (born 11 September 1764 † 10 November 1764)
- Karl Alexander, 5th Prince of Thurn and Taxis (born 22 February 1770; † 15 July 1827)
- ∞ 25 May 1789 with Duchess Therese of Mecklenburg-Strelitz
- Prince Friedrich Johann Nepomuck of Thurn and Taxis (born 11 April 1772 † 7 December 1805), unmarried

Auguste bore Karl Anselm eight children until 1772. After several assassination attempts by his wife, Karl Anselm banished Auguste in January 1776 to strict house arrest at first to Burg Trugenhofen (later renamed Schloss Taxis) in Dischingen and then to Schloss Hornberg in the Black Forest, where she died on 4 June 1787. The couple legally divorced in 1776. Following the death of his first wife, Karl Anselm married that same year morganatically to Elisabeth Hildebrand.

Acquisition of new territories

Karl Anselm acquired in 1786, the Swabian county of Friedberg-Scheer and had to spend almost the entire proceeds from the Imperial Reichspost. Thereupon the Emperor Joseph II brought the county to "Gefürsteten Grafschaft" status. During the invasion of French troops in the Austrian Netherlands in 1794, the local properties of the Thurn and Taxis family were seized. With the further advance of the French troops, all the possessions of the Thurn and Taxis were lost. To compensate, Karl Anselm was awarded in 1803, according to Article 13 of the Reichsdeputationshauptschluss (formally the *Hauptschluss der außerordentlichen Reichsdeputation*, or "Principal Conclusion of the Extraordinary Imperial Delegation") other Swabian lands, including the Free Imperial City of Buchau, the Imperial Abbey of Buchau, the Imperial Abbeys of Marchtal and Neresheim, Ostrach, and other villages.

Losses within the Reichspost

By 1790, the hereditary fiefs of the Thurn and Taxis family fueled the Imperial Reichspost to its greatest extent. The Austrian Netherlands and Tyrol were added to the Thurn and Taxis postal system. Due to the Napoleonic Wars, Karl Anselm's Imperial Reichspost gradually lost more and more postal districts beginning with the Austrian Netherlands, thus depriving the post of important sources of revenue. With the Treaty of Lunéville formalized on 9 February 1801, the Imperial Reichspost lost all postal districts in the Rhine region. After Prussia had been compensated for the loss of its left-bank territories by right bank areas in May 1802, Prussia took over the sovereignty over the postal services, and so the Imperial Reichspost lost further postal districts. Only under his son and successor, Karl

Alexander, was the Thurn and Taxis family able to re-establish its postal system as the private company Thurn-und-Taxis-Post.

Titles and styles

- **2 June 1733 – 8 November 1739**: *His Serene Highness* Prince Karl Anselm of Thurn and Taxis
- **8 November 1739 – 17 March 1773**: *His Serene Highness* The Hereditary Prince of Thurn and Taxis
- **17 March 1773 – 13 November 1805**: *His Serene Highness* The Prince of Thurn and Taxis

Honours

- Grand Master of the Order of Parfaite Amitié
- Knight of the Austrian Order of the Golden Fleece

Source (edited): "http://en.wikipedia.org/wiki/Karl_Anselm,_4th_Prince_of_Thurn_and_Taxis"

Karl August, 10th Prince of Thurn and Taxis

***Karl August* Joseph Maria Maximilian Lamoral Antonius Ignatius Benediktus Valentin, Prince of Thurn and Taxis**, full German name: *Karl August Joseph Maria Maximilian Lamoral Antonius Ignatius Benediktus Valentin Fürst von Thurn und Taxis* (born 23 July 1898 at Schloss Garatshausen in Feldafing, Kingdom of Bavaria; died 26 April 1982 in Regensburg, Bavaria, Germany) was the tenth Prince of Thurn and Taxis and Head of the Princely House of Thurn and Taxis from 13 July 1971 until his death on 26 April 1982.

Early life and education

Karl August was the third son and child of Albert, 8th Prince of Thurn and Taxis, and his wife Archduchess Margarethe Klementine of Austria. After graduating from a local high school, Karl August studied science at the University of Würzburg.

Marriage and family

Karl August married Princess Maria Anna of Braganza, daughter of Miguel, Duke of Braganza, and his wife Princess Maria Theresa of Löwenstein-Wertheim-Rosenberg, on 18 August 1921 at Schloss Taxis in Dischingen, Baden-Württemberg, Germany. Karl August and Maria Ana had four children:

- Princess Clotilde of Thurn and Taxis (30 November 1922-1 September 2009)
- Princess Mafalda of Thurn and Taxis (6 March 1924-24 July 1989)
- Johannes, 11th Prince of Thurn and Taxis (5 June 1926 – 28 December 1990)
- Prince Albert of Thurn and Taxis (23 January 1930 – 4 February 1935)

After his marriage, Karl August and his wife resided at Gut Höfling in Regensburg where he managed the family's agricultural interests in nearby Burgweinting. As a committed opponent to Nazism, Karl August forbade his children, after the Machtergreifung, to join the Hitler Youth.

World War II

Because of his anti-Nazi attitude, Karl August was imprisoned in a Gestapo prison in Landshut from 1944 to 1945. After the death of his older brother Franz Josef in 1971, Karl August was aged 73 when he ascended to become Head of the House of Thurn and Taxis. During this time, he was responsible for the modernization of the agricultural and forestry possessions of the House of Thurn and Taxis and built homes for his workers and employees. In addition, he supported the continued preservation of the cultural-historical heritage of the House of Thurn and Taxis. Karl August restored interior parts of St. Emmeram's Abbey as well as tapestries from the 17th and 18th centuries. After his death on 26 April 1982, Karl August was entombed in the chapel of St. Emmeram's Abbey.

Titles, styles, honours and arms

Titles and styles

- **23 July 1898 – 13 July 1971**: *His Serene Highness* Prince Karl August of Thurn and Taxis
- **13 July 1971 – 26 April 1982**: *His Serene Highness* The Prince of Thurn and Taxis

Honours

- Grand Master of the Order of Parfaite Amitié
- Knight Grand Cross of the Order of St. Sylvester

Source (edited): "http://en.wikipedia.org/wiki/Karl_August,_10th_Prince_of_Thurn_and_Taxis"

Margravine Sophie Christine of Brandenburg-Bayreuth

Margravine *Sophie Christine* Louise of Brandenburg-Bayreuth (in German: *Sophie Christine Luise, Markgräfin von Brandenburg-Bayreuth*; 4 January 1710, Schloss Weferlingen, Weferlingen– 13 June 1739, Brussels, Austrian Netherlands) was a member of the Brandenburg-Bayreuth line of the House of Hohenzollern and a Margravine of Brandenburg-Bayreuth by birth. Through her marriage to Alexander Ferdinand, 3rd Prince of Thurn and Taxis, Sophie Christine was also a member of the Princely House of Thurn and Taxis and Hereditary Princess consort of Thurn and Taxis.

Family and early life

Sophie Christine was the eldest child and daughter of George Frederick Charles, Margrave of Brandenburg-

Bayreuth and his first wife Princess Dorothea of Schleswig-Holstein-Sonderburg-Beck.

Marriage and issue

Sophie Christine married Alexander Ferdinand, Hereditary Prince of Thurn and Taxis, the eldest child and only son of Anselm Franz, 2nd Prince of Thurn and Taxis and his wife Maria Ludovika Anna Franziska, Princess of Lobkowicz, on 11 April 1731 in Frankfurt am Main. Sophie Christine and Alexander Ferdinand had five children:
- Princess Sophie Christine of Thurn and Taxis (baptized 8 December 1731 † 23 December 1731)
- Karl Anselm, 4th Prince of Thurn and Taxis (born 2 June 1733 † 13 November 1805) ∞ 3 September 1753 Duchess Auguste of Württemberg (30 October 1734-4 June 1787) ∞ 1787 Elisabeth Hildebrand, Frau von Train
- Princess Luise Auguste Charlotte of Thurn and Taxis (born 27 October 1734 † January 1735)
- Prince Friedrich August of Thurn and Taxis (baptized 5 December 1736 † 12 September 1755)
- Prince Ludwig Franz Karl Lamoral Joseph of Thurn and Taxis (born 13 October 1737 † 7 August 1738)

Titles and styles

- **4 January 1710 – 11 April 1731**: *Her Serene Highness* Margravine Sophie Christine of Brandenburg-Bayreuth
- **11 April 1731 – 13 June 1739**: *Her Serene Highness* The Hereditary Princess of Thurn and Taxis, Margravine of Brandenburg-Bayreuth

Source (edited): "http://en.wikipedia.org/wiki/Margravine_Sophie_Christine_of_Brandenburg-Bayreuth"

Maria Theresia Ahlefeldt

Maria Theresia Ahlefeldt (born **Princess *Maria Theresia* of Thurn and Taxis**, [full German name: *Maria Theresia, Prinzessin von Thurn und Taxis*] 16 January 1755 in Regensburg, Free Imperial City of Regensburg, Holy Roman Empire; died 20 December 1810 in Prague, Kingdom of Bohemia, Austrian Empire) was a member of the House of Thurn and Taxis and a Princess of Thurn and Taxis by birth and a member of the Ahlefeldt Danish noble family and Countess of Ahlefeldt-Langeland through her marriage to Ferdinand, Count of Ahlefeldt-Langeland. Maria Theresia was a Danish (originally German) composer. She is known as the first female composer in Denmark.

Family

Maria Theresia was the eldest child and daughter of Alexander Ferdinand, 3rd Prince of Thurn and Taxis (1704–73) and his third wife Princess Maria Henriette Josepha of Fürstenberg-Stühlingen (1732–72). She was a younger half-sister of Karl Anselm, 4th Prince of Thurn and Taxis and niece of Maria Augusta of Thurn and Taxis.

Early life and marriage

She grew in a cultural environment at the princely court in Regensburg. Maria Theresia was engaged to Prince Joseph of Fürstenberg 1772-76 until her affair with Prince Philip of Hohenlohe. In 1780, she fled arrest after having married the Danish noble Ferdinand, Count of Ahlefeldt-Langeland (1747–1815) against the will of her family.

Career as a composer

In 1780, Maria Theresia's spouse was marshal at the court of Ansbach, where she was active in the amateur theatre. In 1792-94, her spouse was marshal of the Danish court and director of the Royal Danish Theatre. Maria Theresia composed music for several ballets, operas, and plays of the royal theatre. She moved to Dresden in 1798 and lived from 1800 until her death in Prague.

Selection of work

- *La Folie, ou quel Conte!* (libretto) 1780s
- *Telemak paa Calypsos Øe* (music, aria, choir), 1792
- *Veddemaalet* (music), 1793
- *Romance de Nina* 1794/98

Source (edited): "http://en.wikipedia.org/wiki/Maria_Theresia_Ahlefeldt"

Maximilian Anton Lamoral, Hereditary Prince of Thurn and Taxis

Maximilian Anton Lamoral, **Hereditary Prince of Thurn and Taxis**, full German name: *Maximilian Anton Lamoral Erbprinz von Thurn und Taxis* (born 28 September 1831 in Regensburg, Kingdom of Bavaria; died 26 June 1867 in Regensburg, Kingdom of Bavaria) was the Hereditary Prince of Thurn and Taxis from birth until his death in 1867.

Marriage and family

Maximilian married Duchess Helene in Bavaria, daughter of Duke Maximilian Joseph in Bavaria and his wife Princess Ludovika of Bavaria, on 24 August 1858 at Possenhofen Castle. Helene was the eldest sister of Elisabeth of Bavaria (later Empress of Austria). Maximilian and Helene had four children:
- Princess Louise of Thurn and Taxis (1 June 1859 – 20 June 1948)
- Princess Elisabeth of Thurn and Taxis (28 May 1860 – 7 February 1881)
- Maximilian Maria, 7th Prince of Thurn and Taxis (24 June 1862 – 2 June 1885)
- Albert, 8th Prince of Thurn and Taxis (8 May 1867 – 22 January 1952)

The marriage of Maximilian and Helene

did not take place without difficulty as Maximilian II of Bavaria refused to allow his first cousin to marry a prince that was not of a royal house. Franz Joseph I of Austria and his wife Elisabeth of Bavaria intervened and the marriage took place as planned. Franz Joseph was originally intended to marry Helene, but fell in love with and married her sister Elisabeth instead.

Death

Maximilian died of either kidney failure or lung paralysis on 26 June 1867 at the age of 35 in Regensburg. He was interred in the burial chapel at St. Emmeram's Abbey. Due to his early death, his son Maximilian Maria became Hereditary Prince of Thurn and Taxis and ultimately the princely house's seventh Prince.

Ludwig II of Bavaria wrote in a personal letter of condolence to Maximilian's father, Maximilian Karl: "I sympathize with your loss the deep pain and just the same and the whole Taxis family feels and discretion very well what a lot of hopes with the dear passing away of life is extinguished."

Titles and styles
- **28 September 1831 – 26 June 1867**: *His Serene Highness* The Hereditary Prince of Thurn and Taxis

Honours
- Knight of the Austrian Order of the Golden Fleece (1862)

Source (edited): "http://en.wikipedia.org/wiki/Maximilian_Anton_Lamoral,_Hereditary_Prince_of_Thurn_and_Taxis"

Maximilian Karl, 6th Prince of Thurn and Taxis

Maximilian Karl, **Prince of Thurn and Taxis**, full German name: *Maximilian Karl Fürst von Thurn und Taxis* (born 3 November 1802 in Regensburg, Electorate of Bavaria; died 10 November 1871 in Regensburg, Kingdom of Bavaria) was the sixth Prince of Thurn and Taxis, head of the Thurn-und-Taxis-Post, and Head of the Princely House of Thurn and Taxis from 15 July 1827 until his death on 10 November 1871.

Early life, education, and military career

Maximilian Karl was the fourth child of Karl Alexander, 5th Prince of Thurn and Taxis and his wife Duchess Therese of Mecklenburg-Strelitz, sister of Louise of Mecklenburg-Strelitz. He was born on 3 November 1802 in the so-called Inner Palace of St. Emmeram's Abbey. At the age of nine, Maximilian Karl became Under Lieutenant in Bayer's Fourth Bayerrischen Cheveaulegers-Regiment König. After four years of education at Bildungsinstitut Hofwyl, a Swiss educational institution, he joined the Bavarian army on 25 August 1822. After the death of his father in 1827, Maximilian Karl asked for his dismissal from the army. Afterwards, he continued with his new role as head of the House of Thurn and Taxis, with the advisement and support of his mother.

Marriage and family

Maximilian Karl married Baroness Wilhelmine of Dörnberg, daughter of Ernst, Baron of Dörnberg and his wife Baroness Wilhelmine Henriette Maximiliane of Glauburg, on 24 August 1828 in Regensburg. Maximilian Karl and Wilhelmine had five children:
- Prince Karl Wilhelm of Thurn and Taxis (14 April 1829 – 21 July 1829)
- Princess Therese Mathilde of Thurn and Taxis (31 August 1830 – 10 September 1883)
- Maximilian Anton Lamoral, Hereditary Prince of Thurn and Taxis (28 September 1831 – 26 June 1867)
- Prince Egon of Thurn and Taxis (17 November 1832 – 8 February 1892)
- Prince Theodor of Thurn and Taxis (9 February 1834 – 1 March 1876)

Maximilian Karl and Mathilde Sophie with their family at the occasion of their silver wedding anniversary on 24 January 1864.

In their seventh year of marriage, Wilhelmine died at the age of 32. Maximilian Karl mourned her death greatly and constructed the Neo-Gothic mausoleum at St. Emmeram's Abbey for her. Maximilian Karl married secondly to Princess Mathilde Sophie of Oettingen-Oettingen and Oettingen-Spielberg, daughter of Johannes Aloysius III, Prince of Oettingen-Oettingen and Oettingen-Spielberg and his wife Princess Amalie Auguste of Wrede, on

24 January 1839 in Oettingen in Bayern. Maximilian Karl and Mathilde Sophie had twelve children:
- Prince Otto of Thurn and Taxis (28 May 1840 – 6 July 1876)
- Prince Georg of Thurn and Taxis (11 July 1841 – 22 December 1874)
- Prince Paul of Thurn and Taxis (27 May 1843 – 10 March 1879)
- Princess Amalie of Thurn and Taxis (12 May 1844 – 12 February 1867)
- Prince Hugo of Thurn and Taxis (24 November 1845 – 15 May 1873)
- Prince Gustav of Thurn and Taxis (23 February 1848 – 9 July 1914)
- Prince Wilhelm of Thurn and Taxis (20 February 1849 – 11 December 1849)
- Prince Adolf of Thurn and Taxis (26 May 1850 – 3 January 1890)
- Prince Franz of Thurn and Taxis (2 March 1852 – 4 May 1897)
- Prince Nikolaus of Thurn and Taxis (2 August 1853 – 26 May 1874)
- Prince Alfred of Thurn and Taxis (11 June 1856 – 9 February 1886)
- Princess Marie Georgine of Thurn and Taxis (25 December 1857 – 13 February 1909)

In 1843, Maximilian Karl and his family moved to the newly constructed princely castle of the Thurn and Taxis family in Donaustauf, which was completed in the same year as the nearby Walhalla. The castle Donaustauf was completely destroyed during a blaze on 4 March 1880.

Postal career

In 1827, Maximilian Karl was his father's successor as head of the private Thurn-und-Taxis-Post which had its headquarters in Frankfurt am Main. With the annexation of the Free City of Frankfurt by the Kingdom of Prussia in 1866 and the forced sale of Thurn-und-Taxis-Post against compensation ended the era of the Thurn and Taxis family's postal monopoly. The handover took place on 1 July 1867.

Titles and styles

- **3 November 1802 – 13 November 1805**: *His Serene Highness* Prince Maximilian Karl of Thurn and Taxis
- **13 November 1805 – 15 July 1827**: *His Serene Highness* The Hereditary Prince of Thurn and Taxis
- **15 July 1827 – 10 November 1871**: *His Serene Highness* The Prince of Thurn and Taxis

Honours

- Grand Master of the Order of Parfaite Amitié
- Knight of the Austrian Order of the Golden Fleece
- Knight of the Order of the Black Eagle

Source (edited): "http://en.wikipedia.org/wiki/Maximilian_Karl,_6th_Prince_of_Thurn_and_Taxis"

Maximilian Maria, 7th Prince of Thurn and Taxis

Maximilian Maria Carl Joseph Gabriel Lamoral, **Prince of Thurn and Taxis**, full German name: *Maximilian Maria Carl Joseph Gabriel Lamoral Fürst von Thurn und Taxis* (born 24 June 1862 at Schloss Taxis in Dischingen, Kingdom of Württemberg; died 2 June 1885 in Regensburg, Bavaria, Germany) was the seventh Prince of Thurn and Taxis and Head of the Princely House of Thurn and Taxis from 10 November 1871 until his death on 2 June 1885.

Early life

Maximilian Maria was the eldest of the two sons of Maximilian Anton Lamoral, Hereditary Prince of Thurn and Taxis and Duchess Helene in Bavaria. After the death of his father on 26 June 1867, he became heir apparent to the headship of the House of Thurn and Taxis. With the death of his grandfather Maximilian Karl, 6th Prince of Thurn and Taxis on 10 November 1871, he succeeded as Prince of Thurn and Taxis at the age of nine.

Education

To prepare for his future office, Maximilian Maria received his education from Baron Carl von Geyr-Schleppenburg. Maximilian Maria attended no public school, but was given private lessons. Beginning in the Autumn of 1880, he studied philosophy, law, and economics at the Universities of Bonn, Strasbourg, and Göttingen. Since his youth, he was fascinated not only with riding and hunting, but also with the promotion of arts and sciences. He urged his archivist to establish and write a scientifically-based history of the House of Thurn and Taxis.

Career and philanthropy

To celebrate his achievements and the official takeover of the government business of the House of Thurn and Taxis, Maximilian Maria created generous foundations for the poor of the city of Regensburg and the surrounding countryside, and also for the restoration of the St. Emmeram's Abbey.

Death

He died very young. His heart had been weakened by scarlet fever in childhood, and he suffered from severe heart spasms. In 1885, he died of a pulmonary embolism.

Titles, styles, honours and arms

Titles and styles

- **24 June 1862 – 26 June 1867**: *His Serene Highness* Prince Maximilian Maria of Thurn and Taxis
- **26 June 1867 – 10 November 1870**: *His Serene Highness* The Hereditary Prince of Thurn and Taxis
- **10 November 1870 – 2 June 1885**: *His Serene Highness* The Prince of Thurn and Taxis

Honours

- Grand Master of the Order of Parfaite Amitié
- Knight of the Austrian Order of the Golden Fleece

Source (edited): "http://en.wikipedia.org/wiki/Maximilian_Maria,_7th_Prince_of_Thurn_and_Taxis"

Order of Parfaite Amitié

The Order of Parfaite Amitié (German: *Orden de Parfaite Amitié*) is a dynastic order of knighthood and a house order of chivalry in the Princely House of Thurn and Taxis.

History

The Order was created during the reign of Alexander Ferdinand, 3rd Prince of Thurn and Taxis as the supreme order of the princely house. Karl Anselm, 4th Prince of Thurn and Taxis then reformed the Order and was able to formally transmit the Order to descendants to this day. With the abolition of the principalities of the Confederation of the Rhine by the acts of 12 July 1806, the Order's value became related to the dynasty, and is be given to members who have turned 18 years of age.

Design

The Order's medal consists of a golden eight-pointed Maltese cross in white enamel. Within the arms of the cross is located a tower and an upright lion, the symbol from the coat of arms of the House of Thurn and Taxis. In the shame arm of the cross are engraved the words *VINICULUM AMICITAE* (Latin: *chain of friendship*). In the medallion are the initials CA (Carl Anselm). Marked blue-enamelled medallion with the letters or TW Since 1928, the initial A (Albert).

Men wear the decoration around their neck with sky-blue band. A copy of the Order is in the treasury at the museum at St. Emmeram's Abbey in Regensburg.
Source (edited): "http://en.wikipedia.org/wiki/Order_of_Parfaite_Amiti%C3%A9"

Prince Gabriel of Thurn and Taxis

Prince *Gabriel* Albert Maria Michael Franz Joseph Gallus Lamoral of Thurn and Taxis (German: *Gabriel Albert Maria Michael Franz Joseph Gallus Lamoral Prinz von Thurn und Taxis*) (16 October 1922- 17 December 1942) was a member of the Princely House of Thurn and Taxis and a Prince of Thurn and Taxis. Gabriel was second in the line of succession to the Headship of the House of Thurn and Taxis after his father Franz Joseph, Hereditary Prince of Thurn and Taxis until his death in the Battle of Stalingrad, at which point he was replaced by his uncle Prince Karl August of Thurn and Taxis.

Gabriel was born at Schloss Haus near Regensburg, Bavaria, the eldest child and son of Prince Franz Joseph of Thurn and Taxis (later 9th Prince of Thurn and Taxis) and his wife Princess Isabel Maria of Braganza. His twin brother, Prince Michaele of Thurn and Taxis, died at birth. Gabriel was a paternal grandson of Albert, 8th Prince of Thurn and Taxis and his wife Archduchess Margarethe Klementine of Austria and a maternal grandson of Miguel, Duke of Braganza and his wife Princess Maria Theresa of Löwenstein-Wertheim-Rosenberg.

World War II

During World War II, Gabriel was conscripted for military service before completing high school. He served first as a Gefreiter (Private First Class) and then as an officer in the Wehrmacht. Gabriel was serving in a Reiter-Regiment (Cavalry Regiment) in the Wehrmacht when he was killed in action at the Battle of Stalingrad on 17 December 1942. He was interred among the unknown dead at the war cemetery at Rossoschka.

Titles, styles, honours and arms

Titles and styles

- **16 October 1922 – 17 December 1942**: *His Serene Highness* Prince Gabriel of Thurn and Taxis

Source (edited): "http://en.wikipedia.org/wiki/Prince_Gabriel_of_Thurn_and_Taxis"

Prince Gustav of Thurn and Taxis

Prince *Gustav* Franz Maria of Thurn and Taxis, full German name: *Gustav Franz Maria, Prinz von Thurn und Taxis* (born 22 August 1888 in Dresden, Kingdom of Saxony; died 30 April 1919 in Munich, Bavarian Soviet Republic), was a member of the House of Thurn and Taxis and a Prince of Thurn and Taxis by birth. As a member of the Thule Society, Gustav was killed by the Bavarian Soviet Republic (German: *Bayerische Räterepublik*) government during the German Revolution of 1918–19.

Family

Gustav was the fourth child and second son of Prince Franz of Thurn and Taxis and his wife Countess Theresia Grimaud of Orsay. Through his father, Gustav was a grandson of Maximilian Karl, 6th Prince of Thurn and Taxis and his wife Princess Mathilde Sophie of Oettingen-Oettingen and Oettingen-Spielberg.

Thule Society

Gustav was a member of the Thule Society (German: *Thule-Gesellschaft*), a German occultist and völkisch group in Munich, named after a mythical northern country from Greek legend.

German Revolution

As White Guard (German: *Weisse Garde*) forces (a coalition of Prussian and

Bavarian troops combined with Freikorps) surrounded Munich, the Communists began to raid nationalist strong points throughout the city. On 26 April 1919, the Red Army (German: *Rote Armee*) broke into the Thule Society premises and arrested secretary Countess Heila von Westarp, Gustav, and five other members, labelling them as "right-wing spies." Gustav and the other hostages were taken to the cellar of the Luitpold Gymnasium, which had served as a Red Army post since mid-April. The seven Thule Society members, including Gustav, and three Freikorps soldiers were killed on 30 April as a reprisal for reports of the killing of Red soldiers by Whites at Starnberg. Gustav and his fellow hostages were lined up against a wall and executed by a firing squad. Their deaths may have also been a reprisal for an attempt by Thule Society members to infiltrate the Bavarian Soviet Republic's government and stage a coup d'état on 30 April. Gustav was the most notable of the four titled members killed in the incident, due to his family's extensive ties with several of Europe's royal houses.

Vatican nuncio Eugenio Pacelli (the later Pope Pius XII) referred to the fights and the murder of the hostages in an article in the newspaper "*Bayerischer Kurier*" (founded in 1856) on October 1st 1919:

"The Nunciature itself was riddled with bullets during the fights between communists and republican government troops. Armed spartacists entered here with force, and when I protested against the violation of international law I was threatened with a gun. I know in what gruesome manner the hostages were murdered."

Titles and styles

- **22 August 1888 – 30 April 1919**: *His Serene Highness* Prince Gustav of Thurn and Taxis

Honours

- Knight of the Order of Parfaite Amitié

Source (edited): "http://en.wikipedia.org/wiki/Prince_Gustav_of_Thurn_and_Taxis"

Prince Gustav of Thurn and Taxis (1848–1914)

Prince Gustav of Thurn and Taxis (bottom right) together with his family at the occasion of the silver wedding anniversary of his parents on 24 January 1864.

Prince *Gustav* Otto Maximilian Lamoral of Thurn and Taxis (1848–1914), full German name: *Gustav Otto Maximilian Lamoral Prinz von Thurn und Taxis*, was the sixth child of Maximilian Karl, 6th Prince of Thurn and Taxis and his second wife Princess Mathilde Sophie of Oettingen-Oettingen and Oettingen-Spielberg. He was born on 2 February 1848 in Regensburg, Kingdom of Bavaria.

Family

Paul, one of his elder brothers, was an intimate friend and aide-de-camp of King Ludwig II of Bavaria.

Marriage

On 8 September 1877, Gustav married Princess Karoline of Thurn and Taxis, daughter of Hugo Maximilian Prince of Thurn and Taxis and Almeria Countess of Belcredi, in Lautschin, Austria-Hungary. The couple did not have any children.

Later life

From 1882 to 1888, he was *Bezirkshauptmann* of Bregenz, Vorarlberg, Austria-Hungary, where he died at the age of 66 on 9 July 1914.

In 1884, Prince Gustav acquired the *Villa Güllich* in Bregenz, which is known today as *Palais Thurn & Taxis* with a public park area of about 16000 m, which is heritage-protected. Since 1984, the Palais also houses an international center for contemporary art.

Source (edited): "http://en.wikipedia.org/wiki/Prince_Gustav_of_Thurn_and_Taxis_(1848%E2%80%931914)"

Prince Ludwig Philipp of Thurn and Taxis

Prince *Ludwig Philipp* Maria Friedrich Joseph Maximilian Antonius Ignatius Lamoral of Thurn and Taxis, full German name: *Ludwig Philipp Maria Friedrich Joseph Maximilian Antonius Ignatius Lamoral, Prinz von Thurn und Taxis*, also *Louis Philippe* (born 2 February 1901 at Regensburg, Kingdom of Bavaria; died 22

April 1933 at Schloss Niederaichbach in Niederaichbach, Bavaria, Germany) was a member of the House of Thurn and Taxis and a Prince of Thurn and Taxis by birth.

Family

Ludwig Philipp was the fourth child and son of Albert, 8th Prince of Thurn and Taxis and his wife Archduchess Margarethe Klementine of Austria.

Ludwig Philipp married Princess Elisabeth of Luxembourg, fifth child and daughter of William IV, Grand Duke of Luxembourg and his wife Infanta Marie Anne of Portugal, on 14 November 1922 in Hohenburg, Bavaria, Germany. Ludwig Philipp and Elisabeth had two children:
- Prince Anselm of Thurn and Taxis (14 April 1924 – 25 February 1944)
- Princess Iniga of Thurn and Taxis (25 August 1925 – 17 September 2008)

Ludwig Philipp of Thurn and Taxis studied law at the Julius-Maximilians University of Würzburg. He was a member of the catholic fraternity KDStV Cheruscia Würzburg (Cartellverband der katholischen deutschen Studentenverbindungen).

Titles, styles, honours and arms

Titles and styles

- **2 February 1901 – 22 April 1933**: *His Serene Highness* Prince Ludwig Philipp of Thurn and Taxis

Honours

- Knight of the Order of Parfaite Amitié

Source (edited): "http://en.wikipedia.org/wiki/Prince_Ludwig_Philipp_of_Thurn_and_Taxis"

Prince Max Emanuel of Thurn and Taxis

For his nephew, see Prince Max Emanuel of Thurn and Taxis (b. 1935).

Prince *Max Emanuel* Maria Siegfried Joseph Antonius Ignatius Lamoral of Thurn and Taxis (German: *Max Emanuel Maria Siegfried Joseph Antonius Ignatius Lamoral, Prinz von Thurn und Taxis*) (born 1 March 1902 in Regensburg, Kingdom of Bavaria; died 3 October 1994 in Regensburg, Bavaria, Germany), known as **Father Emmeram** (German: *Pater Emmeram*), was a German Benedictine and member of the Princely House of Thurn and Taxis.

Early life

Max Emanuel was the fourth eldest son of Albert, 8th Prince of Thurn and Taxis and his wife Archduchess Margarethe Klementine of Austria. He had six brothers and one sister. Max Emanuel's eldest brother was Franz Joseph, 9th Prince of Thurn and Taxis.

Monastic life

Max Emanuel joined the Order of Saint Benedict in 1923 and became a member of Neresheim Abbey. For his religious name, he chose *Emmeram* after Saint Emmeram of Regensburg.

In 1951, Max Emanuel received the papal concession for the reestablishment of the former monastery Prüfening Abbey. Later in the 1950s, he established the *Liturgiewissenschaftliche Institut Regensburg-Prüfening* (German: *Liturgic Scientific Institute Regensburg-Prüfening*). For over 30 years of his life, Max Emanuel resided isolated at the family-owned St. Emmeram's Abbey in Regensburg. His desire to revive the monastic life was not fulfilled, however, so he opened Prüfening Abbey as a meeting place and home for the youth and poor. Max Emanuel died in 1994 and was buried at Neresheim Abbey.

Titles, styles, honours and arms

Titles and styles

- **1 March 1902 – 3 October 1994**: *His Serene Highness* Prince Max Emanuel of Thurn and Taxis

Honours

- Knight of the Order of Parfaite Amitié

Source (edited): "http://en.wikipedia.org/wiki/Prince_Max_Emanuel_of_Thurn_and_Taxis"

Prince Max Emanuel of Thurn and Taxis (b. 1935)

For his uncle and namesake, see Prince Max Emanuel of Thurn and Taxis.

Prince Max Emanuel of Thurn and Taxis (born 7 September 1935) is the heir presumptive to Albert, 12th Prince of Thurn and Taxis, who as of 2010 is still unmarried and childless. Max Emanuel belongs to Germany's richest princely family, whose wealth derives from founding the German postal service and brewing.

Marriage and issue

On 20 May 1969 at Schwangau, Max Emanuel entered into a civil morganatic marriage with Countess Anna Maria von Poccii, a daughter of Count Konrad Albert von Poccii and his wife Elisabeth Hartmann. They married in a religious ceremony two days later. A childless marriage, they divorced a year later, on 1 July 1970 at Kempten; the marriage was annulled on 17 October 1972 at Augsburg.

On 14 March 1973 at Schwangau, he entered into another morganatic union, civilly marrying Christa Ingeburg Heinle, a daughter of Erich Heinle and his wife Ingeburg Wurzner. The following day, they had a religious ceremony. He and Christa have two sons; as both are the issue of an unequal union, they have no claims to the throne of Thurn and Taxis:
- Prince Hubertus Raphael Franz Josef Ulrich Maria Lamoral von Thurn und Taxis (b. 22 Jun 1973)
- Prince Philipp Gabriel Franz Josef

Magnus Maria Lamoral von Thurn und Taxis (b. 19 Apr 1975)

Building plan tensions

Max Emanuel's plans in the late 1990s and early 2000s to develop real estate near historical sites in Bavaria caused tensions with historical societies and others in the local community. The prince already had a commercial presence in the area, as he ran a "sport and seminar" center which offered river rafting, mountain biking, paragliding, and a little bit of golf.

In 1997, Max Emanuel planned to build a $22 million luxury hotel with 150 rooms, fine dining, a golf school and adjacent golf course, and a health spa on land directly in view of Neuschwanstein Castle, the famous site built by Ludwig II of Bavaria. These preparations were defeated however, after locals and a conservation society managed to get a local referendum held in 1997 to scrap the plans. Max Emanuel continued his plans four years later to build a hotel and golf course on the same site. People living nearby were upset that the view seen from the castle's grounds would be ruined by new construction meant for tourists; consequently the local council ruled that most of the land surrounding the castle was unusable for commercial development. Max Emanuel responded to these complaints by saying a luxury hotel would draw wealthy visitors to the village and help the local economy; restaurant, shop owners, and other members of the tourist industry tended to favor his plans, while village counselors, local farmers and others were opposed, believing that any commercial development would ruin the rural landscape and create too much noise. Those in favor of King Ludwig's legacy stated that the hotel would violate the romantic legacy the mad king left.

A bureaucratic mistake during initial plans four year previously left one piece of land available for commercial development in 2001, a fact that Prince Max was able to take advantage of. With a seat on the council as a Christian Social Union member, he proceeded with plans for a scaled-down leisure complex of 50 rooms and a six-hole golf training course, which the Bavarian state parliament ruled to be legal. Critics complained that even these plans would impede the views of the castle, as it would be easy for further construction to continue building the site up. As a result of these new plans, efforts were quickly underway by various groups, such as the Bavarian Society for the Protection of Nature, to declare the castle and surrounding land a world heritage site.

Max Emanuel and his family stated that if the plans were not approved, they would be forced to sell Schloss Bullachberg (the property in the shadow of the castle) as well as a nearby ancestral castle that required restoration; many saw this announcement as a barely concealed threat: if their plans were rejected, these properties might be sold to another developer with even more unpleasant plans for the area.

Construction plans still remain in limbo today; in 2006, Porsche Automobil Holding SE acquired the property, intending to continue the project.

Titles, styles, honours and arms

Titles and styles

- **7 September 1935 – present**: *His Serene Highness* Prince Max Emanuel of Thurn and Taxis

Honours

- Knight of the Order of Parfaite Amitié

Source (edited): "http://en.wikipedia.org/wiki/Prince_Max_Emanuel_of_Thurn_and_Taxis_(b._1935)"

Prince Paul of Thurn and Taxis

Paul Maximilian Lamoral, **Prince of Thurn and Taxis**, full German name: *Paul Maximilian Lamoral Fürst von Thurn und Taxis*, was the third child of Maximilian Karl, 6th Prince of Thurn and Taxis and his second wife Princess Mathilde Sophie of Oettingen-Oettingen and Oettingen-Spielberg. He was born on 27 May 1843 in Castle Donaustauf near Regensburg, and died on 10 March 1879 in Cannes, France, where he was buried at the Cimetière du Grand Jas, Allée du Silence no. 33 under the name of *Paul de Fels*.

Friendship with Ludwig II of Bavaria

At the request of his father to King Maximilian II of Bavaria, he was appointed on 15 November 1861 as junior lieutenant in the 2nd Bavarian artillery regiment (military registry no. KA OP 69 547) and was assigned as orderly officer of then Crown Prince Ludwig on 1 May 1863. Ludwig and Paul became close friends after spending three weeks together in Berchtesgaden in September 1863. After Ludwig's accession to the throne in 1864, Paul was promoted to personal aide-de-camp of the king on 18 January 1865. In the following two years, Paul von Thurn und Taxis, who matched the king in his good looks, became the closest friend and confidant of the monarch, who gave him the nickname *Faithful Friedrich*:

"Let me assure you that I shall always foster with the same sincerity the feelings of gratefulness and faithful love which I bear for you in my heart. Remember with love, your faithful Ludwig" (Letter of Ludwig II to Paul).

Although this infatuation, like that with Richard Wagner, was probably not sexually expressed, there were rumours in Munich that Ludwig was sexually intimate with his aide-de-camp.

Paul appears to have kept a diary, but like everything else concerning him in the Regensburg archives of the Thurn und Taxis family, it has been destroyed. Following letter was sent by Paul to Ludwig from his apartment at Türkenstrasse 82 in Munich on 5 May 1866:

"Dear and Beloved Ludwig! I am just finishing my diary with the thought of the beautiful hours which we spent to-

gether that evening a week ago which made me the happiest man on earth... Oh, Ludwig, Ludwig, I am devoted to you! I couldn't stand the people around me; I sat still and, in my thought I was with you...How my heart beat when, as I passed the Residenz, I saw a light in your window."

Prince Paul of Thurn and Taxis as Lohengrin.

Paul and Ludwig shared their passion for Richard Wagner and the theatre. He was gifted with a beautiful voice and sang before the King several times. Wagner rehearsed with Paul a part of the opera Lohengrin which was performed at the occasion of the 20th birthday of the king on August 25, 1865 at the Alpsee in Hohenschwangau. It was magnificently staged with Paul - dressed as Lohengrin wearing a silver shining armor - drawn over the lake by an artificial swan and the whole scenery was illuminated by electric light.

After Richard Wagner was forced to leave Munich on 10 December 1865, Prince Paul of Taxis served as a discreet messenger and intermediary between Ludwig and Wagner. Ludwig apparently also toyed with the idea of abdicating in order to follow his hero into exile, but Wagner with the assistance of Taxis dissuaded him from doing so, while both of them stayed incognito at Wagner's Villa in Tribschen in May 1866. Using the alias ''Friedrich Melloc'', Paul travelled again to Tribschen on 6 August 1866, this time, however without Ludwig, obviously to convince Wagner to return to Munich. Paul's following letter to Ludwig is dated 7 August 1866:

"I have just left the intimate circle of the Dear Friends (i.e. Richard & Cosima Wagner) and have retired to the cosy little room which we shared when we were here together... Beautiful memory!...He and Frau Vorstal (i.e. Richard & Cosima Wagner) send their deepest greetings. May God protect you and keep you on the Throne. This is their wish and my own, because only then can we achieve our high ideal. The results of my mission are best given verbally, and I believe that you will approve of them....But now good night, in my thoughts I salute you a thousand times. Your sincere and faithful Friedrich."

Prince Paul of Thurn and Taxis.

But soon the relationship between Paul and Ludwig soured. Jealous tongues attempted to discredit Paul, and evil and untrue rumours reached Ludwig's ears that Paul lived a frivolous life. Having little malice in his own nature, Ludwig could never get used to it in others and at first he probably took the rumours about Paul at face value.

Although Ludwig's feelings for his friend grew deeper and developed into great love, the friendship was so precariously balanced that the slightest tremor of reality threatened to send it plummeting to oblivion. Paul again "faltered" making a wrong choice, saying the wrong word, displaying too much familiarity on one occasion and not enough affection on another. Trivial in themselves, such incidents preyed upon Ludwig's mind until they became unbearable. Once and for all, he cut Paul out of his life. Apparently the final indiscretion was so trivial that even Paul himself was unaware of it. When he learned of his fall from grace, he sent some agonized letters to the King, but there was to be no response from Ludwig. Paul's letter to Ludwig is undated, but must have been written somewhere about the middle of December 1866:

"My own beloved Ludwig! What in the name of all the Saints has your Friedrich done to you? What did he say that no hand, no good night, no Auf Wiedersehen favoured him? How I feel I cannot say, my trembling hand may show you my inner disquiet. I did not intend to hurt you. Forgive me; be good again with me, I fear the worst - I cannot stand this. May my notes climb to you reconcilingly. Amen! Forgive your unhappy Friedrich".

Marriage, Break-up with his Family and Death

Prince Paul of Thurn and Taxis (top) together with his family at the occasion of the silver wedding anniversary of his parents on 24 January 1864.

On 7 November 1866, Paul is released from his duties as aide-de-camp and transferred to an artillery regiment "*under gracious recognition of his services*". From midst November 1866, he started to drink without limits and in a state of turmoil and distress ended up with the Jewish soubrette Elise Kreuzer of the Actien-Volkstheater, "*with whom he spend a night at a local boarding house, he was well too drunk to remember, the next morning they parted but in the end of December 1866 she proclaimed him to be the father of her unborn child*".

After their final break up Paul would never see Ludwig again. In January 1867, Paul retired from the Bavarian army under peculiar circumstances, which were later termed as "desertion" by Minister of War Siegmund von Pranckh in 1872. Using the alias "Rudolphi", Paul moved to Wankdorf near Bern, Switzerland, together with Elise where their son Heinrich, named after Elise's father Heinrich Kreuzer, a known opera singer, was born on 30 June 1867.

After Paul received notice that his parents had tasked the Bavarian police to trace their son in order to convince him to abandon Elise, they moved to Mannheim or Ludwigshafen in August 1867. In October 1867, Paul took up an engagement at the municipal theatre of Aachen under the name "Herr von Thurn" together with Elise.

1867 was a very challenging year for the Thurn and Taxis family. Paul's sister Amalie died on 12 February 1867 at the age of 22 and his half-brother, Maximilian Anton Lamoral, the Hereditary Prince of Thurn and Taxis, passed away on 26 June 1867 at the age of 36. With the annexation of the Free City of Frankfurt am Main - where the Thurn-und-Taxis-Post had its headquarters - by the Kingdom of Prussia in 1866 during the Austro-Prussian war, the era of the Thurn and Taxis family's postal monopoly ended on 1 July 1867 with the handover to Prussia.

In 1868, Prince Paul von Thurn und Taxis was forced by his family to marry Elise morganatically, and thereafter was disowned by them, stripped of all his titles, rank and birthrights against an annual pension of 6000 florin. Paul kept writing to Ludwig but without any reply, in the end he begged the King to give him a title. On 19 June 1868 Ludwig inscribed him upon the list of the nobility of Bavaria as *Herr Paul von Fels*. However, his later petition for conferment of hereditary nobility was declined on 10 December 1869 at the request of the Bavarian Ministry.

Paul tried to reconnect with Richard Wagner as a diary entry of Cosima Wagner on 11 April 1869 shows: "*...Hans reporting nothing but bad things from Munich; on top of that a letter from Paul of Fels (formerly Prince Taxis), who wants an appointment of some kind, and, in order to secure it, tells us a lot of gossip! At three o'clock a boat trip with the three little ones and R.*"

Paul started a new attempt to reconcile with his father and visited him together with Elise on 3 August 1869 in castle Donaustauf, obviously to no avail. Paul became then an actor at the Zurich theatre in Switzerland, however, ended his acting career after being hissed off the stage.

After his father died on on 10 November 1871, his sister-in-law, Helene of Thurn and Taxis, became the unofficial head of the family until her son, Maximilian Maria, the Hereditary Prince, became of age on 24 June 1883. Known for her diplomatic skills, she tried to reconnect Paul to King Ludwig II and, according to newspaper reports of 1874, Paul would regain his family name and become the *Marshall of the Royal Palace Herrenchiemsee* and *Master of the Revels* to King Ludwig II. However, this was not realized for unknown reasons.

In 1877/78, Elise was the prima donna at the theatre of Freiburg. According to Baring-Gould she "*exacted from her husband that, whenever she acted, he should throw a bouqet on to the stage at her feet, and get his friends to do the same*".

Shortly after, Paul came down with tuberculosis and went with his wife to Lugano, where he grew worse. Elise formed a liaison with a Prussian officer, staying at the same hotel, and eloped with him, '"*leaving her husband, who had given up so much for her, to die unbefriended*" on March 10, 1879 in Cannes, "*remembering the only true love of his life*".

In 1879, Paul's widow - under the name of Frau Elisabeth von Fels - joined the Municipal Theatre in Lübeck together with Arno Cabisius, whom she married in 1881. In 1891, Cabisius became the Director of the Magdeburg Municipal Theatre which he led until his death on 6 March 1907. Elisabeth Cabisius-Kreuzer took over the directorship to complete her husband's contract until the end of the season 1907/08. The fate of Paul's son Heinrich von Fels, who was left behind with his father after Elise abandoned her family, remains unclear.

Trivia

- In the TV series *Wagner* (1983) with Richard Burton as Richard Wagner and Vanessa Redgrave as Cosima

Wagner, Prince Paul of Thurn and Taxis (played by Arthur Denberg) appears performing as Lohengrin on the Alpsee and at the occasion of his visit to Tribschen together with King Ludwig II in May 1866.
- Prince Paul Taxis is featured as lover of King Ludwig II in the three-volume manga series *Ludwig II (Rutovihi II sei)* by the artist You Higuri, published by Kadokawa Shoten.

Titles, styles, honours and arms

Titles and styles
- **27 May 1843 – 7 June 1868**: *His Serene Highness* Prince Paul of Thurn and Taxis
- **7 June 1868 – 10 March 1879**: Paul, Lord of Fels

Honours
- Knight of the Order of Parfaite Amitié

Source (edited): "http://en.wikipedia.org/wiki/Prince_Paul_of_Thurn_and_Taxis"

Princess Christa of Thurn and Taxis

Princess *Christa* Ingeborg of Thurn and Taxis, full German name: *Christa Ingeborg, Prinzessin von Thurn und Taxis* (born 14 December 1941 in Heidenheim an der Brenz, Baden-Württemberg, Germany) is the current president of the Bavarian Red Cross (BRK) and a member of the Princely House of Thurn and Taxis.

Marriage and issue
Christa married Prince Max Emanuel of Thurn and Taxis, only child of Prince Raphael Rainer of Thurn and Taxis and his wife Princess Margarete of Thurn and Taxis, civilly on 14 March 1973 in Schwangau, Bavaria, Germany and religiously on 15 March 1973 at Schloss Bullachberg in Bavaria. Christa and Max Emanuel had two sons:
- Prince Hubertus of Thurn and Taxis (born 22 June 1973)
- Prince Philipp of Thurn and Taxis (born 19 April 1975)

Functionary and honorary positions
Beginning in 1985, Christa was the Bavarian Red Cross (BRK) vice chairman for the district of Ostallgäu and from 1989, for the region of Swabia. Christa served in these positions until 2005. Since 1989, she has been a member of the BRK-Land Board and the Committee for Social Services and since 1994, the Federal Committee for Welfare and Social Work in BRK. From 1993 to 2001, Christa was a member BRK Committee for Readiness and in 1995 she was a founding member of the Academy of the German Red Cross. From 1997 to 2000, she was a senator in the Landtag of Bavaria. In November 1999, Christa began serving as Vice President of BRK. On 8 November 2003, she became the first woman to be elected President of the Bavarian Red Cross; she had already led the organization for the past five months after the previous president scaled down his duties due to health problems. In the same year she was also member of the Council Pen (Stiftsratsvorsitzende Jutta Lowag) of the women's pen on Luitpoldpark in Munich.

Titles and styles
- **14 December 1941 – 14 March 1973**: *Miss* Christa Ingeborg Heinle
- **14 March 1973 – present**: *Her Serene Highness* Princess Christa of Thurn and Taxis

Source (edited): "http://en.wikipedia.org/wiki/Princess_Christa_of_Thurn_and_Taxis"

Princess Elisabeth Helene of Thurn and Taxis

Princess Elisabeth Helene of Thurn and Taxis (German: *Elisabeth Helene, Prinzessin von Thurn und Taxis*) (born 15 December 1903 in Regensburg, Kingdom of Bavaria; died 22 October 1976 in Munich, Bavaria, Germany) was a Princess of Thurn and Taxis by birth and a Princess and Duchess of Saxony, Margravine of Meissen, and titular Queen consort of Saxony through her marriage to Friedrich Christian, Margrave of Meissen. Elisabeth was the sixth child of Albert, 8th Prince of Thurn and Taxis and his wife Archduchess Margarethe Klementine of Austria.

Marriage and issue
Elisabeth married Prince Friedrich Christian of Saxony, second eldest child and son of Frederick Augustus III of Saxony and his wife Archduchess Luise of Austria, Princess of Tuscany, on 16 June 1923 in Regensburg, Bavaria. Elisabeth and Friedrich had five children:
- Maria Emanuel, Margrave of Meissen (born 1926); married Princess Anastasia of Anhalt
- Princess Maria Josepha of Saxony (born 1928)
- Princess Anna of Saxony (born 1929); married Roberto de Afif, Prince of Gessaphe
- Prince Albert of Saxony (born 1934); married Elmira Henke
- Princess Mathilde of Saxony (born 1936); married Prince John Henry of Saxe-Coburg and Gotha

Titles, styles, honours and arms

Titles and styles
- **15 December 1903 – 16 June 1923**: *Her Serene Highness* Princess Elisabeth Helene of Thurn and Taxis
- **16 June 1923 – 18 February 1932**: *Her Royal Highness* Princess Elisabeth Helene of Saxony, Duchess of Saxony, Princess of Thurn and Taxis
- **18 February 1932 – 9 August 1968**: *Her Royal Highness* The Margravine

of Meissen
- *Title in pretence:* **18 February 1932 – 9 August 1968**: *Her Majest* The Queen of Saxony
- **9 August 1968 – 22 October 1976**: *Her Royal Highness* The Dowager Margravine of Meissen

Source (edited): "http://en.wikipedia.org/wiki/Princess_Elisabeth_Helene_of_Thurn_and_Taxis"

Princess Elisabeth of Luxembourg (1901–1950)

Princess *Elisabeth* Marie Wilhelmine of Luxembourg, full French name: *Elisabeth Marie Wilhelmine de Nassau-Weilburg, Princesse de Luxembourg* (born 7 March 1901 in Luxembourg, Grand Duchy of Luxembourg; died 2 August 1950 at Schloss Hohenburg in Hohenburg, Bavaria, Germany) was a member of the House of Nassau-Weilburg and a Princess of Luxembourg by birth and a member of the House of Thurn and Taxis and Princess of Thurn and Taxis through her marriage to Prince Ludwig Philipp of Thurn and Taxis. Two of Elisabeth's elder sisters reigned as sovereign Grand Duchess of Luxembourg and titular Duchess of Nassau: Marie-Adélaïde and Charlotte.

Family

Elisabeth was the fifth-eldest daughter and child of William IV, Grand Duke of Luxembourg and his wife Infanta Marie Anne of Portugal.

Elisabeth married Prince Ludwig Philipp of Thurn and Taxis, fourth child and son of Albert, 8th Prince of Thurn and Taxis and his wife Archduchess Margarethe Klementine of Austria, on 14 November 1922 in Hohenburg, Bavaria, Germany. Elisabeth and Ludwig Philipp had two children:
- Prince Anselm of Thurn and Taxis (14 April 1924 – 25 February 1944)
- Princess Iniga of Thurn and Taxis (25 August 1925 – 17 September 2008)

Titles, styles, honours and arms

Titles and styles

- **7 March 1901 – 14 November 1922**: *Her Grand Ducal Highness* Princess Elisabeth of Luxembourg
- **14 November 1922 – 2 August 1950**: *Her Grand Ducal Highness* Princess Elisabeth of Thurn and Taxis, Princess of Luxembourg

Source (edited): "http://en.wikipedia.org/wiki/Princess_Elisabeth_of_Luxembourg_(1901%E2%80%931950)"

Princess Elisabeth of Thurn and Taxis

Princess Elisabeth of Thurn and Taxis (German: *Elisabeth Maria Maximiliana, Prinzessin von Thurn und Taxis*) (born 28 May 1860 in Dresden, Kingdom of Saxony; died 7 February 1881 in Ödenburg, Austrian Empire)

Life

Elisabeth was a Princess of Thurn and Taxis by birth and an Infanta of Portugal, Princess of Braganza, and titular Queen consort of Portugal through her marriage to Miguel, Duke of Braganza, Miguelist claimant to the throne of Portugal from 1866 to 1920.

Elisabeth was the second eldest child and daughter of Maximilian Anton Lamoral, Hereditary Prince of Thurn and Taxis and his wife Duchess Helene in Bavaria.

Marriage and Issue

Elisabeth married Miguel, Duke of Braganza, only son and second eldest child of Miguel of Portugal and his wife Adelaide of Löwenstein-Wertheim-Rosenberg, on 17 October 1877 in Regensburg, Kingdom of Bavaria.

Elisabeth and Miguel had three children:

- Prince Miguel of Braganza, Duke of Viseu (1878–1923), married Anita Stewart
- Prince Francis Joseph of Braganza (1879–1919)
- Princess Maria Teresa of Braganza (1881–1945), married Prince Karl Ludwig of Thurn and Taxis

The couple moved to Austria, where on 22 September 1878 in Reichenau an der Rax, her first son, Miguel Maximiliano, was born. It was after this birth that Elisabeth's health began to deteriorate. Elisabeth died at the age of 20 in Ödenburg shortly after the birth of her third child, Maria Teresa.

Elisabeth's mother Helene withdrew after her death more and more from public life. Her husband Miguel eventually remarried on 8 November 1893 in Kleinheubach to Princess Maria Theresa of Löwenstein-Wertheim-Rosenberg.

Titles, styles, honours and arms

Titles and styles

- **28 May 1860 – 17 October 1877**: *Her Serene Highness* Princess Elisabeth of Thurn and Taxis
- **17 October 1877 – 7 February 1881**: *Her Royal Highness* The Duchess of Braganza

Source (edited): "http://en.wikipedia.org/wiki/Princess_Elisabeth_of_Thurn_and_Taxis"

Princess Elisabeth von Thurn und Taxis

Princess Elisabeth von Thurn und Taxis (born *Elisabeth Margarethe Maria Anna Beatriz Prinzessin von Thurn and Taxis*) is a princess of the German Thurn und Taxis House. She may have been the first member of nobility to personally write a regular blog, "*The Princess Diaries*", which appeared in the London-based "Finch's Quarterly Review", an online journal about high fashion, the arts and wealthy lifestyles, until October 2010. The blog contrasted her "relative normality" as a writer and editor, living and working in London, with a (sometimes) globetrotting socialite lifestyle. In her final blog entry, she promised a collection of her writings would shortly be published in book form.

Elisabeth was born on 24 March 1982 at Schloss St. Emmeram in Regensburg, the daughter of Gloria, Princess of Thurn and Taxis and Johannes, 11th Prince of Thurn and Taxis.

The Princess has two siblings, an older sister and a younger brother:
- *Maria Theresia* Ludovika Klothilde Helene Alexandra Prinzessin von Thurn und Taxis, born 28 November 1980 in Regensburg
- *Albert* Maria Lamoral Miguel Johannes Gabriel Prinz von Thurn und Taxis, born 24 June 1983 in Regensburg, who succeeded his father in 1990 as Albert II, Prince of Thurn and Taxis.

Elisabeth was educated in England in Sevenoaks, Kent and has a B.A. from the American University of Paris. She has lived in many countries and now resides in North-West London, where according to her blog, she is looking for a new flat.

In her childhood, the princess and her brother and sister were frequent guests of Michael Jackson, something Elisabeth recalled in her blog after his death, in which she strongly defends Jackson's reputation. "I couldn't imagine Michael hurting a fly, let alone a friend."

Elisabeth has frequently featured in socialite diary items and appears as an "heiress" in Vanity Fair's "Fortune's Children" piece in June 2009, photographed by Bruce Weber. "I think it's a huge privilege to be able to use the access that we have in an interesting way" she said, discussing a book about art collectors she is writing in collaboration with Alex Flick.

Elisabeth has written for the British Catholic Herald about the revival of traditional religious communities in France. She signed a 2008 petition asking the bishops of England and Wales to provide more Latin Sunday Tridentine Masses (authorized as an extraordinary form of the Roman Rite by the 2007 motu proprio *Summorum Pontificum*). The Princess was made a Dame of the Order of Malta in 2009, in which capacity she has several times accompanied the disabled and elderly on a pilgrimage to Lourdes.

Elisabeth likes the form of Pilates known as "True Pilates". Speaking on their website, she said "I truly love this form of exercise and recommend it to anyone looking for a balanced workout and a healthy body awareness." She is also fond of kitesurfing and waterskiing.

Blogger and writer

Elisabeth is Features Editor for Finch's Quarterly Review, which is distributed worldwide and was a regular blogger in the journal, which is moving to print-only format, from February 2009 - October 2010. The blog light-heartedly contrasted the expectations, pleasures, difficulties and assumptions surrounding "princess" status with more "normal" issues like flat-hunting, London weather, writing and work. In addition to her blog, Elisabeth also writes freelance for several German and International art and style publications, including New York-based style magazine Quest and German art/culture publication Monopol. Her main writing interest is in the arts and her blog describes many visits to galleries and art exhibitions in various fields, including the Venice Biennale.

A recent liturgical volume written by Princess Elisabeth, with a foreword by the current Pope's elder brother, Georg Ratzinger, *The Faith of Children: in Praise of the People's Devotion* (*La Fede dei Piccoli*) has been published in Italian and German in December 2010. Although the German Federal government does not recognize "noble" or "royal" status per se, members of the former royal, princely, and noble houses of German descent use their "titles" which the German government regards as last names. As a courtesy and for ease of use, female members of these families use the feminized version of the family name. There is no existing monarchical class system in Germany, Austria, or the nations once part of the former Habsburg empires.

Source (edited): "http://en.wikipedia.org/wiki/Princess_Elisabeth_von_Thurn_und_Taxis"

Princess Eugénie of Greece and Denmark

Princess Eugénie (Evgenia) of Greece and Denmark (Greek: Πριγκίπισσα Ευγενία της Ελλάδας και Δανίας) (10 February 1910 – 13 February 1989) was the youngest child and only daughter of Prince George of Greece and Denmark and his wife, Marie Bonaparte, daughter of Prince Roland Bonaparte. Her father was the second son of George I of Greece and Olga, Queen of Greece.

Marriage and issue

She married Prince Dominic Radziwiłł on 30 May 1938 in Paris. They divorced in 1946. They had two children:
- Princess *Tatiana* Maria Renata Eugenia Elisabeth Margarete

Radziwiłł (b. 28 August 1939) married Jean Henri Fruchaud
- Fabiola Fruchaud (b. 7 February 1967), married Thierry Herman; one daughter Tatiana; one son, Edouard (2007) with Didier Fradin (1959).
- Alexis Fruchaud (b. 25 November 1969) married Natalie Chandler, one daughter, Thalia Tatiana Eugenie Lily Marie {b. 23 June 2008}.
- Prince Jerzy (George) Andreas Dominicus Heironymus Peter Leon Radziwiłł (4 November 1942 – 27 August 2001)

Eugénie remarried on 28 November 1949 to Prince Raymundo della Torre e Tasso, Duke of Castel Duino. Their marriage also ended in divorce, in 1965. They had one son:
- Prince Carlo Alessandro, Duke of Castel Duino (b. 10 February 1952), married to Veronique Lantz, three children.
  - Dimitri (b. 1977)
  - Maximilian (b. 1979)
  - Constanza (b. 1989).

Titles, styles, honours and arms

Titles and styles

- **10 February 1910 – 30 May 1938**: *Her Royal Highness* Princess Eugénie of Greece and Denmark
- **30 May 1938 – 28 November 1949**: *Her Royal Highness* Princess Dominic Radziwiłł
- **28 November 1949 – 11 May 1965**: *Her Royal Highness* The Duchess of Castel Duino
- **11 May 1965 – 13 February 1989**: *Her Royal Highness* Eugénie, Duchess of Castel Duino

Source (edited): "http://en.wikipedia.org/wiki/Princess_Eug%C3%A9nie_of_Greece_and_Denmark"

Princess Eulalia of Thurn and Taxis

Princess Eulalia Maria Antoine Eleonore of Thurn and Taxis, also known as **Illa**, (21 December 1908 - 30 December 1993) was the eldest child of Prince Friedrich Lamoral of Thurn and Taxis and his wife Princess Eleonore de Ligne. She belonged to the Czech branch of the House of Thurn and Taxis.

Family and early life

Princess Eulalia of Thurn and Taxis was born on 21 December 1908 to the Czech branch of the House of Thurn and Taxis. She was born and raised at the Schloss Biskuptiz in Czechoslovakia. Though her official name was Eulalia, everyone in her family referred to her as "Illa".

Marriage

Engagement to Prince Raphael

Princess Illa was engaged to Prince Raphael Ranier of Thurn and Taxis, a younger son of Albert, 8th Prince of Thurn and Taxis from 1928 to the following year. He belonged to the main branch of the House of Thurn and Taxis, as he was a descendant of Karl Anselm, 4th Prince of Thurn and Taxis. When it came time for the wedding in February 1929, Illa changed her mind and refused to marry him. Her timing meant that the bishop of Regensburg, as well as all of the guests, were all assembled and ready to attend the wedding before her announcement was made. She went to her fiance's father and declared that her "heart belonged to" Prince Philipp Ernst of Thurn and Taxis, his youngest son, and that she found it "incompatible with the dictates of her conscience" to marry her fiance. Albert subsequently consulted her paternal grandfather, who was the head of the Czech branch, and the two next summoned a family council. Both branches of the family involved said they commended Illa for her candor and courage, and also credited her with "the sincerest motivations springing from a deep religious conviction that it would be wrong to marry Prince Raphael when she really loved Prince Philippe". After informing Prince Albert, she apparently "burst into hysterical sobbing" and left soon after for her estates in Czechoslovakia. Her decision was not officially announced until the following day.

Illa had met the two brothers at about the same time, and "the wisdom of an alliance" between herself and Prince Raphael seemed clear. In the week leading up to the wedding however, Illa spent time with Philipp daily and grew feelings for him while staying at the Regensburg home of his and her fiance's parents. A devout Catholic, Illa's "deep religious conviction" would not allow her to trap herself in a marriage with someone she did not love. Prince Raphael later married to another relative, his second cousin Princess Margarete of Thurn and Taxis; the couple were the parents of Prince Max Emanuel, the current heir presumptive to the Thurn and Taxis throne.

Marriage to Prince Phillip

On 7 May 1929, the engagement of Illa to Prince Philipp Ernst of Thurn and Taxis, her former fiance's youngest brother, was formally announced. Their engagement had been tentatively approved until Philipp became of age, and he received his father's blessing before the betrothal was announced; the couple planned on a September wedding.

On 8 September 1929, Illa married Prince Philipp Ernst at the Schloss Taxis. They had three children:
- Prince Albrecht Friedrich Maria Lamorel Kilian of Thurn and Taxis (5 Jul 1930); married Baroness Alexandra von der Ropp, no issue. Their marriage is considered unequal by Thurn and Taxis family law.
- Princess Marguerite Eleonore Marie Franziska Antoine de Padua of Thurn and Taxis (1 Dec 1933)
- Princess Antonia Maria Margareta Theresia vom Kinde Jesu of Thurn and Taxis (28 Jan 1936)

Later life

Illa's father was murdered on 10 May 1945 at Schloss Biskupitz.

Prince Philipp died on 23 July 1964 at the age of 56 at the Schloss Hohenberg in Bavaria. Princess Illa died on 30 December 1993 at the age of 85.

Titles, styles, honours and arms

Titles and styles

- **21 December 1908 – 8 September 1929**: *Her Serene Highness* Princess Eulalia of Thurn and Taxis
- **8 September 1929 – 30 December 1993**: *Her Serene Highness* Princess Philipp Ernst of Thurn and Taxis

Source (edited): "http://en.wikipedia.org/wiki/Princess_Eulalia_of_Thurn_and_Taxis"

Princess Iniga of Thurn and Taxis

Princess *Iniga* Anna Margarete Wilhelmine Luise of Thurn and Taxis, full German name: *Iniga Anna Margarete Wilhelmine Luise, Prinzessin von Thurn und Taxis* (born 25 August 1925 at Schloss Niederaichbach in Niederaichbach, Bavaria, Germany; died 17 September 2008 in Aufhausen, Bavaria, Germany) was a member of the House of Thurn and Taxis and a Princess of Thurn and Taxis by birth and a member of the House of Württemberg and a Princess of Urach and Countess of Württemberg through her marriage to Prince Eberhard of Urach.

Family

Iniga was the second child and only daughter of Prince Ludwig Philipp of Thurn and Taxis and his wife Princess Elisabeth of Luxembourg.

Marriage and issue

Iniga married Prince Eberhard of Urach, eighth child and youngest son of Wilhelm, 2nd Duke of Urach and his wife Duchess Amalie in Bavaria, civilly on 18 May 1948 in Niederaichbach, Bavaria, Germany and religiously on 20 May 1948 in Regensburg, Bavaria, Germany. Prince Eberhard served as a reconnaissance officer in 1938-44 and was promoted to Major. Iniga and Eberhard had five children:

- Princess Amelie of Urach (born 6 April 1949)
- Princess Elisabeth of Urach (born 10 December 1952)
- Karl Anselm, Duke of Urach (born 5 February 1955)
- Wilhelm Albert, Duke of Urach (born 9 August 1957)
- Prince Inigo of Urach (born 12 April 1962)

After her father's death, Iniga inherited her father's estate Schloss Niederaichbach.

Death

Iniga died on 17 September 2008 at her home in Aufhausen. A requiem and funeral were held at the Wallfahrtskirche St. Maria Himmelfahrt in Aufkirchen am Starnberger See on 23 September 2008.

Titles, styles, honours and arms

Titles and styles

- **25 August 1925 – 18 May 1948**: *Her Serene Highness* Princess Iniga of Thurn and Taxis
- **18 May 1948 – 17 September 2008**: *Her Serene Highness* Princess Iniga of Urach, Countess of Württemberg, Princess of Thurn and Taxis

Source (edited): "http://en.wikipedia.org/wiki/Princess_Iniga_of_Thurn_and_Taxis"

Princess Isabel Maria of Braganza

Princess Isabel Maria of Braganza, Infanta of Portugal (sabel Maria Alberta Josefa Micaela Gabriela Rafaela Francisca de Paula e de Assis Teresa Adelaide Eulália Sofia Carolina; 19 November 1894 in Kleinheubach, Kingdom of Bavaria; died 12 January 1970 in Regensburg, Bavaria, Germany) was a member of the House of Braganza and a Princess of Braganza and Infanta of Portugal by birth. Through her marriage to Franz Joseph, 9th Prince of Thurn and Taxis, Isabel Maria was also a member of the House of Thurn and Taxis and Princess consort of Thurn and Taxis.

Family

Isabel Maria was the daughter and child of Miguel, Duke of Braganza and his wife Princess Maria Theresa of Löwenstein-Wertheim-Rosenberg. Her father was the Miguelist claimant to the throne of Portugal from 1866 to 1920.

Isabel Maria married Franz Joseph, Hereditary Prince of Thurn and Taxis, eldest son of Albert, 8th Prince of Thurn and Taxis and his wife Archduchess Margarethe Klementine of Austria, on 23 November 1920 in Bronnbach, Wertheim am Main, Baden-Württemberg, Germany. Isabel Maria and Franz Joseph had five children:

- Prince Gabriel of Thurn and Taxis (16 October 1922 – 17 December 1942)
- Prince Michaele of Thurn and Taxis (16 October 1922 – 17 October 1922)
- Princess Helene of Thurn and Taxis (27 May 1924 – 27 October 1991)
- Princess Maria Theresia of Thurn and Taxis (10 September 1925 – 27 April 1997)
- Princess Maria Ferdinande of Thurn and Taxis (born 19 December 1927)

Titles, styles, honours and arms

Titles and styles

- **19 November 1894 – 23 November 1920**: *Her Royal Highness* Princess Isabel Maria of Braganza, Infanta of Portugal
- **23 November 1920 – 22 January 1952**: *Her Royal Highness* The Hereditary Princess of Thurn and Taxis, Princess of Braganza, Infanta of Portugal
- **22 January 1952 – 12 January 1970**: *Her Royal Highness* The Princess of Thurn and Taxis, Princess of Braganza, Infanta of Portugal

Source (edited): "http://en.wikipedia.org/wiki/Princess_Isabel_Maria_of_Braganza"

Princess Lida of Thurn and Taxis

Lida, Princess Victor of Thurn and Taxis (née **Lida Eleanor Nicolls**), also referred to as **Princess Lida of Thurn and Taxis**, (1875 – 6 December 1965) was an American millionairess, socialite, and the wife of Prince Victor of Thurn and Taxis. She was well-known for her involvement in several highly publicized legal disputes, making her a fixture in newspapers such as *The New York Times*. The first such dispute was with former New York showgirl Josephine Moffitt, who claimed to be the legal spouse of Prince Victor using the name "Josephine, Princess of Thurn and Taxis" and the second was with Bernard Francis S. Gregory, who sued her for $50,000, alleging she had slandered him.

Early life

Born **Lida Eleanor Nicolls** in 1875 in Uniontown, Pennsylvania, she was the daughter of grocer John A. Nicolls and his wife Lenora T. Nicolls. She was a niece of Josiah V. Thompson, a Pittsburgh banker, and coal & fuel operator.

First marriage

In 1899, she met her first husband, General Gerald Purcell Fitzgerald of Ireland. Fitzgerald was a nephew of Edward FitzGerald, a poet famous for his translation of Omar Khayyám's *Rubaiyat of Omar Khayyam* from Persian into English. He had relocated to Fayette County, Pennsylvania to try his hand at the coal industry, where he laid out the coal town of Shamrock near New Salem. They married in Los Angeles, California, late in 1899.

In 1906, she obtained a divorce from Fitzgerald in Irish courts. British law required an Act of Parliament to make their separation final. According to Lida, Fitzgerald treated her with "great cruelty." In her petition to Parliament, Lida recounted how Fitzgerald "dragged your subject out of bed in the middle of the room and she had to scream for help", and how at the Van Nuys Hotel in Los Angeles, he "seized and shook your subject most violently until her hat fell off and her hair fell down." Parliament passed the "Fitzgerald's Divorce (Ireland) Act" in 1907. In Pittsburgh, Lida was awarded an alimony settlement of $20,000 per year and $300,000 in trust for two sons from the marriage, John Fitzgerald and Gerald Purcell Fitzgerald, Jr.

Second marriage

Lida married Prince Victor Theodore Maximilian Egon Maria Lamoral of Thurn and Taxis, third and youngest child of Prince Egon of Thurn and Taxis and his wife Viktoria Edelspacher de Gyoryok, in a wedding ceremony at the home of her mother and presided over by the Reverend Mr. Spence on 1 November 1911 in Uniontown. The couple had arrived from England the previous Friday. Prior to the marriage, Lida was reportedly said to possess $1 million in her own right. Following her marriage to Prince Victor, Lida announced that she and her husband would reside in Europe and she would never again return to the United States. Lida and Prince Victor later registered their marriage in Baltisar, Austria-Hungary in February 1912, where Prince Victor was a citizen by virtue of his father Prince Egon having become naturalized at the time of his marriage to his wife Viktoria Edelspacher de Gyoryok.

Jewelry robbery and wrongful arrest of Kid McCoy

While staying at a hotel in Ostend, Belgium, in July 1912, Lida was robbed of jewelry valued at $80,000. The robbery was thought to have been committed by "a gang of international sharpers" who were staying at the same hotel as Lida. However, American boxer Norman Selby (better known as "Kid McCoy") was arrested at the Hotel Cecil in London on 27 July 1912 on an extradition request by Belgian police in connection with the disappearance of the jewelry. Selby was taken before the Bow Street Police Court Magistrate where he was remanded without bail. After the warrant for his arrest was read to him, Selby responded, "I know nothing whatever about it." He was incarcerated in Brixton Jail in London, where he wrote his own version of a "Ballad of Brixton Jail". He returned to New York City on 1 September 1912 aboard the American oceanliner SS *St. Louis* from Southampton. Selby instructed his solicitor to commence a suit against the government of Belgium for $250,000 for his "wrongful arrest" which he claimed "ruined [his] European business". "I did not know that there was such a person in the world as the Princess of Thurn and Taxis when I went to Ostend to spend the week-end", Selby said.

According to *Le Matin*, a French detective on the staff of M. Hamard conducted an investigation at the hotel which led him to suspect three "gentlemen" from London who occupied rooms next to Lida's apartments. The investigation found that the three gentlemen had formed a "gang of smart hotel thieves" and had intentionally taken rooms near those of Lida intending to take an amount of jewelry valued between $1 and $1.5 million. One of Lida's necklaces alone was reportedly worth $400,000, but the robbers were only able to abscond with a few pieces of jewelry lying on her dressing table.

Identity dispute with Josephine Moffitt

Josephine Moffitt (occasionally spelled Moffatt), who styled and titled herself "Her Royal Highness Josephine, Princess of Thurn and Taxis" and "Princess Josphine de la Tour et Taxis", claimed in the United Kingdom that she was the legal wife of Lida's husband Prince Victor. Moffitt was embroiled in another highly publicized legal case against her "old friend and admirer" James Henry Maur heard in the Westminster Police Court and known popularly as "the Thurn and Taxis blackmailing case." Moffitt alleged that she and Prince Victor had wed at a midnight marriage ceremony at Rector's, New York. As early as March 1908, Prince Victor had informed *The New York Times* that its story of his marriage to Moffitt was "absolutely false."

On 31 January 1914, Lida's solicitor applied for and obtained an issue of writ in the Court of Chancery asking for an injunction against Moffitt to restrain her from using the title "Princess of Thurn and Taxis" and from referring to herself as the wife of Prince Victor of Thurn and Taxis. Lida then traveled to London in February 1914 to defend her marriage and title against Moffitt's claims in person. In addition to settling the legality of her marriage to Prince Victor, Lida also sought to restore her reputation which had been blemished by Moffitt's conduct in "meeting men for supper parties and theatres."

In an interview with *The New York Times* on 15 February 1914 in her suite at London's Carlton Hotel, Lida presented her marriage certificate as proof of her marriage to Prince Victor. Lida was awarded damages, trial costs, an injunction against Moffitt, and a verdict for $500. The Court of Chancery also ruled that Lida, and not Moffitt, was entitled to the title "Princess Victor of Thurn and Taxis".

On 28 January 1915, Lida was awarded a verdict of £250 ($1,250) in damages against *The Daily Sketch* in London after the newspaper published photographs of Lida and Moffitt asking the question, "Who Is Princess Thurn and Taxis?"

Slander dispute with Bernard Francis S. Gregory

Following the outbreak of World War I, Lida's husband Prince Victor was called to serve as an officer in the Austro-Hungarian Army causing Lida to return to the United States. Shortly before Lida was to sail to Europe to rejoin her husband in the Austrian Republic, Bernard Francis S. Gregory, known as "Count Gregory", filed a lawsuit against her for $50,000 in damages on 8 May 1920 in the New York Supreme Court alleging she had made false statements about him which had caused him to be "shunned by social circles" in New York City. Gregory received the order from Justice Robert Paul Lydon shortly after he learned from Lida's son Gerald Fitzgerald, Dr. Stewart Hastings, and Prince Herman of Saxe-Weimar that she was soon returning to Europe.

Gregory alleged in his complaint that in January or February 1920 at the Hotel Netherland in New York City, Count Rudolf Festetics overheard Lida telling others that Gregory was "a thief and a swindler and had tried to swindle her out of $10,000 by trying to put through a milk deal that was a swindle." He also alleged that Lida said Gregory was "not a gentleman, but an imposter, was dishonorable, and had been a coachman in England, and was a very bad man." As a result of these statements, Gregory claimed he had "been seriously injured in [his] good name and fame among [his] friends and acquaintances, and in social circles in which [he had] been accustomed to move [he had] been shunned and avoided by [his] friends." Gregory further stated that he was no longer invited to dinners and social functions "among the best families in New York" and that he had been "ostracized and excluded from the best society."

Later life

Following the death of her husband Prince Victor in Vienna on 28 January 1928, Lida lived between residences in Uniontown, Pennsylvania, New York City, and Europe, however, she continued to maintain a residence at the corner of West Main Street and South Mt. Vernon Avenue in Uniontown.

Lida's life continued to consist of further legal disputes regarding alimony and family matters. On 19 April 1937, Lida went to Federal court in Pittsburgh demanding an accounting from trustees of alimony and trust funds held for her and her son. She claimed the trustees had been negligent in collecting the money and interest of the trust funds which totalled $772,779.

An Internal Revenue Service (IRS) appeals board in Washington, D.C. ruled on 12 January 1938 that Lida owed no back income taxes on amounts she received under an agreement with her first husband at the time of their divorce settlement in 1907. The appeals board further ruled that alimony payments to a former spouse were considered a "household expense" and therefore could not be deducted on income tax returns.

Lida and her son John Purcell Fitzgerald carried their appeal against the trustees of two trust funds in their names at the Second National Bank to the United States Supreme Court on an injunction restraining them from proceeding in the United States District Court for the Western District of Pennsylvania.

She was later also entangled in a lengthy court battle in which she attempted to have the marriage of one of her adult sons annulled.

Death and estate settlement

Following several years of hospitalization, she died in New York City at the age of 90 on 6 December 1965, intestate. In November 1972, Judge James A. Reilly issued a decree, which approved the final accounting of Lida's million-dollar estate and ordered that it be divided between her two surviving sons: Gerald Purcell Fitzgerald, Jr. of New York City and Edward Purcell Fitzgerald of Titusville, New Jersey. At its final accounting, Lida's estate totaled $1,288,123.40, leaving a balance of $659,333.31 after taxes. Her possessions included residences, properties, cash, stocks and bonds, valuable antique furniture, Venetian glass, paintings and statuary, china, porcelain, silver, and two wardrobes full of fur coats. Many of Lida's valuables were stored for years in a downtown Uniontown warehouse and some had been in storage in a London warehouse since the closing of her home there in 1914. Most of the valuables were sold at auction in 1966.

Source (edited): "http://en.wikipedia.org/wiki/Princess_Lida_of_Thurn_and_Taxis"

Princess Louise of Thurn and Taxis

Princess Louise of Thurn and Taxis (German: *Luisa Mathilde Wilhelmine Marie Maximiliane, Prinzessin von Thurn und Taxis*) (born 1 June 1859 at Schloss Taxis in Dischingen, Kingdom of Württemberg; died 20 June 1948 in Sigmaringen, Germany)

Life

Louise was a member of the House of Thurn and Taxis by birth and through her marriage to Prince Frederick of Hohenzollern-Sigmaringen, a Princess of Hohenzollern-Sigmaringen.

Louise was the eldest child of Maximilian Anton Lamoral, Hereditary Prince of Thurn and Taxis and his wife Duchess Helene in Bavaria.

Marriage

Louise married Prince Frederick of Hohenzollern-Sigmaringen, fifth child and youngest son of Charles Anthony, Prince of Hohenzollern and his wife Princess Josephine of Baden, on 21 June 1879 in Regensburg.

Louise and Frederick did not have children.

Titles, styles, honours and arms

Titles and styles

- **1 June 1859 – 21 June 1879**: *Her Serene Highness* Princess Louise of Thurn and Taxis
- **21 June 1879 – 20 June 1948**: *Her Serene Highness* Princess Louise of Hohenzollern, Princess of Thurn and Taxis

Source (edited): "http://en.wikipedia.org/wiki/Princess_Louise_of_Thurn_and_Taxis"

Princess Maria Anna of Braganza

Princess *Maria Ana* Rafaela Micaela Gabriela Lourença of Braganza, Infanta of Portugal, full Portuguese name: *Maria Ana Rafaela Micaela Gabriela Lourença, Princesa de Bragança, Infanta de Portugal* (3 September 1899 – 23 June 1971) was a member of the House of Braganza and a Princess of Braganza and Infanta of Portugal by birth. Through her marriage to Karl August, Hereditary Prince of Thurn and Taxis, Maria Ana was also a member of the House of Thurn and Taxis and Hereditary Princess consort of Thurn and Taxis.

Family

Maria Anna was born at Schloss Fischhorn in Zell am See, Salzburg, Austria–Hungary, the daughter and child of Miguel, Duke of Braganza and his wife Princess Maria Theresa of Löwenstein-Wertheim-Rosenberg. Her father was the Miguelist claimant to the throne of Portugal from 1866 to 1920.

Marriage and issue

Maria Anna married Prince Karl August of Thurn and Taxis, third eldest son of Albert, 8th Prince of Thurn and Taxis and his wife Archduchess Margarethe Klementine of Austria, on 18 August 1921 at Schloss Taxis in Dischingen, Baden-Württemberg, Germany. Maria Anna and Karl August had four children:

- Princess Clotilde of Thurn and Taxis (born 30 November 1922)
- Princess Mafalda of Thurn and Taxis (born 6 March 1924)
- Johannes, 11th Prince of Thurn and Taxis (5 June 1926 – 28 December 1990)
- Prince Albert of Thurn and Taxis (23 January 1930 – 4 February 1935)

Princess Maria Anna died in Feldafing, Bavaria, Germany.

Titles, styles, honours and arms

Titles and styles

- **3 September 1899 – 18 August 1921**: *Her Royal Highness* Princess Maria Anna of Braganza, Infanta of Portugal
- **18 August 1921 – 23 June 1971**: *Her Royal Highness* Princess Maria Anna of Thurn and Taxis, Princess of Braganza, Infanta of Portugal

Source (edited): "http://en.wikipedia.org/wiki/Princess_Maria_Anna_of_Braganza"

Princess Maria Augusta of Thurn and Taxis

Princess Maria Augusta Anna of Thurn and Taxis (11 August 1706 – 1 February 1756) was a Regent of Württemberg. She was a member of the Princely House of Thurn and Taxis as a daughter of Anselm Franz, 2nd Prince of Thurn and Taxis and his wife Maria Ludovika Anna Franziska, Princess of Lobkowicz. Through her marriage to Karl Alexander, Duke of Württemberg, she became **Duchess consort of Württemberg**.

Early life

Maria Augusta was born on 11 August 1706. She grew up in the Austrian Netherlands and later moved to Frankfurt, where her family's wealth and economic interests were based. Her only brother was Alexander Ferdinand, 3rd Prince of Thurn and Taxis, whose son Karl Anselm would marry Maria Augusta's only daughter in 1753.

Marriage and children

Maria Augusta was chosen as a bride for Karl Alexander, Duke of Württemberg-Winnental (later Duke of Württemberg) because of her Roman Catholic religion. They were married on 1 May 1727 in Frankfurt am Main. They had four surviving children:
- Karl Eugen, Duke of Württemberg (1728–1793), married Elisabeth Fredericka Sophie of Brandenburg-Bayreuth; no issue.
- Eugen Louis (1729)
- Louis Eugene, Duke of Württemberg (1731–1795), married Sophie Albertine of Beichlingen; had issue.
- Frederick II Eugene, Duke of Württemberg (1732–1797), married Friederike Dorothea of Brandenburg-Schwedt; had issue.
- Alexander Eugen (1733–1734)
- Auguste Elisabeth (1734–1787), married Karl Anselm, 4th Prince of Thurn and Taxis; had issue.

Their ten-year marriage was turbulent, and they were generally felt to be each other's match in every way (as both were masters of intrigue and secret diplomacy). He often used a trusted servant to spy on his wife to ensure that she would not interfere in government or criticize the Duke's ministers. After a particularly serious dispute in 1736, her husband even had her promise in writing to stay out of government affairs.

Regent

Maria Augusta's husband died suddenly on 12 March 1737 on the eve of his departure on a military inspection tour. This meant that their nine year old son Karl Eugen succeeded as Duke of Württemberg. After experiencing initial trouble from the regency council in trying to hold power for her son, she was finally successful on 5 November 1737. She was granted a large allowance and was recognized as co-regent with control over her son's education.

Maria Augusta's eldest son Karl Eugen

From 1739 to the following year, she had an affair with a captain in the army. Rumors of a possible pregnancy became so widespread that the privy council began an investigation; the captain was discharged and she was forced to stay in Brussels for five months (beginning in April 1740). Her exile removed her from direct power, especially when crucial policy decisions and preparations for her son's education were being made. For instance, she was unable to prevent a disastrous alliance with Prussia that would leave Württemberg exposed at the outbreak of the War of the Austrian Succession.

By 1744 however, Maria Augusta had again achieved a position of considerable influence. She arranged military careers for her two eldest sons, allowing them to receive commissions in the Prussian army. In 1748, she encouraged her eldest son the reigning Duke Karl Eugen to enter into a marriage with the Hohenzollern Elisabeth Fredericka Sophie of Brandenburg-Bayreuth, a niece of Frederick the Great. As a Catholic, she prepared her youngest son Frederick Eugen for a life in the Imperial Church. Her dreams for a life of religion for him fell apart however when he became engaged to another niece of Frederick the Great, Friederike Dorothea of Brandenburg-Schwedt in 1753; he also became one of Frederick's most important cavalry commanders.

Maria Augusta's influence would decline as her son grew increasingly more independent by 1749. She died on 1 February 1756 in Göppingen, Württemberg.

Personal attributes

Maria Augusta was often praised by contemporaries for her beauty. In addition, she was also often criticized for her lack of judgment and resolve however. This criticism most likely stemmed from the fact that she liked to breach the contemporary norms of a consort and involve herself in the affairs of government.

She also liked to openly demonstrate her rank as Duchess of Württemberg by spending lavishly, which set her at odds with her thrifty subjects. For instance, her wardrobe contained 228 dresses; the most expensive cost 500 florins, which was more than 30 times a servant's annual income. Although often portrayed as an intellectual lightweight, she owned a large library that contained the latest novels, plays, and philosophy. She also maintained a correspondence with Voltaire.

Titles, styles, honours and arms

Honours
- Dame Grand Cross of the Order of Saint John

Source (edited): "http://en.wikipedia.org/wiki/Princess_Maria_Augusta_of_Thurn_and_Taxis"

Princess Maria Sophia of Thurn and Taxis

Princess *Maria Sophia* Dorothea Caroline of Thurn and Taxis (full German name: *Maria Sophia Dorothea Caroline, Prinzessin von Thurn und Taxis*) (born 4 March 1800 in Regensburg, Free Imperial City of Regensburg, Holy Roman Empire; died 20 December 1870 in Regensburg, Kingdom of Bavaria) was a member of the House of Thurn and Taxis and a Princess of Thurn and Taxis by birth and a member of the House of Württemberg and a Duchess of Württemberg through her marriage to Duke Paul Wilhelm of Württemberg, a German naturalist and explorer.

Family

Maria Sophia was the fifth child and fourth daughter of Karl Alexander, 5th Prince of Thurn and Taxis and his wife Duchess Therese of Mecklenburg-Strelitz. She was a younger sister of Maximilian Karl, 6th Prince of Thurn and Taxis and Maria Theresia, Princess Esterházy of Galántha.

Marriage and issue

Maria Sophia married Duke Paul Wilhelm of Württemberg, fifth and youngest child of Duke Eugen of Württemberg and his wife Princess Luise of Stolberg-Gedern., on 17 April 1827 in Regensburg. Maria Sophia and Paul Wilhelm had one son:

- Duke Wilhelm Ferdinand *Maximilian* Karl of Württemberg (Schloss Taxis 3 September 1828 – Regensburg 28 July 1888), married Princess Hermine of Schaumburg-Lippe, eldest child of Adolf I, Prince of Schaumburg-Lippe

Maria Sophia and Paul Wilhelm divorced on 2 May 1835. Following her divorce, Maria Sophia acquired Württembergisches Palais and its adjacent Herzogspark in Regensburg. She made her residence at the Württembergisches Palais until her death.

Titles, styles, honours and arms

Titles and styles

- 4 March 1800 – 17 April 1827: *Her Serene Highness* Princess Maria Sophia of Thurn and Taxis
- 17 April 1827 – 20 December 1870: *Her Royal Highness* Duchess Maria Sophia of Württemberg, Princess of Thurn and Taxis

Source (edited): "http://en.wikipedia.org/wiki/Princess_Maria_Sophia_of_Thurn_and_Taxis"

Princess Maria Theresia of Thurn and Taxis (1794–1874)

Princess *Maria Theresia* of Thurn and Taxis, full German name: *Maria Theresia, Prinzessin von Thurn und Taxis* (born 6 July 1794 in Regensburg, Free Imperial City of Regensburg, Holy Roman Empire; died 18 August 1874 in Hütteldorf, Penzing, Vienna, Austria–Hungary) was a member of the House of Thurn and Taxis and a Princess of Thurn and Taxis by birth and a member of the House of Esterházy and Princess Esterházy of Galántha from 25 November 1833 to 21 May 1866 through her marriage to Paul III Anthony, 8th Prince Esterházy of Galántha.

Family

Maria Theresia was the third child and second daughter of Karl Alexander, 5th Prince of Thurn and Taxis and his wife Duchess Therese of Mecklenburg-Strelitz. She was an elder sister of Maximilian Karl, 6th Prince of Thurn and Taxis.

Marriage and issue

Maria Theresia married Prince Paul Anthony Esterházy of Galántha, eldest child and son of Nicholas II, 7th Prince Esterházy of Galántha and his wife Princess Maria Josepha of Liechtenstein, on 18 June 1812 in Regensburg, Kingdom of Bavaria. Maria Theresia and Paul Anthony had three children:

- Princess Maria Theresia Esterházy of Galántha (27 May 1813 – 14 May 1894)
- Princess Theresia Rosa Esterházy of Galántha (12 July 1815 – 28 February 1894)
- Nicholas III, 9th Prince Esterházy of Galántha (25 June 1817 – 28 January 1894)

Esterházy was a popular diplomat and Maria Theresia became admired by his contemporaries, especially during the Congress of Vienna.

Titles, styles, honours and arms

Titles and styles

- 6 July 1794 – 18 June 1812: *Her Serene Highness* Princess Maria Theresia of Thurn and Taxis
- 18 June 1812 – 25 November 1833: *Her Serene Highness* The Hereditary Princess Esterházy of Galántha, Princess of Thurn and Taxis
- 25 November 1833 – 21 May 1866: *Her Serene Highness* The Princess Esterházy of Galántha, Princess of Thurn and Taxis
- 21 May 1866 – 18 August 1874: *Her Serene Highness* The Dowager Princess Esterházy of Galántha, Princess of Thurn and Taxis

Source (edited): "http://en.wikipedia.org/wiki/Princess_Maria_Theresia_of_Thurn_and_Taxis_(1794%E2%80%931874)"

Princess Maria Theresia of Thurn and Taxis (b. 1980)

Princess *Maria Theresia* **Ludowika Klothilde Helene Alexandra of Thurn and Taxis**, full German name: *Maria Theresia Ludowika Klothilde Helene Alexandra, Prinzessin von Thurn und Taxis* (born 28 November 1980 in Regensburg, Bavaria, Germany) is a member of the Princely House of Thurn and Taxis and a Princess of Thurn and Taxis. Along with her siblings, Maria Theresia is a forest and agricultural landowner and manager of one of Europe's largest private estates. Maria Theresia rose to prominence in 2001 when the *Neue Post* claimed she was to marry the Spanish crown prince, Felipe, Prince of Asturias.

Maria Theresia is the eldest child and daughter of Johannes, 11th Prince of Thurn and Taxis and his wife Countess Mariae Gloria of Schönburg-Glauchau. Maria Theresia's family's lands form one of the largest private estates in Europe. After the death of her father in 1990, Maria Theresia was a joint heir, along with her sister Princess Elisabeth von Thurn und Taxis and Albert, 12th Prince of Thurn and Taxis, to one of the largest privately-owned forests in Europe, consisting of 36,000 hectares. She and her siblings are the largest private landowners in Germany.

Early life and education

Maria Theresia attended elementary school and secondary school in Regensburg where she lived with her family at Schloss St. Emmeram. To acquire her qualification for university entrance (German: *Hochschulreife*), Maria Theresia's mother shielded her from the German media by sending her to England to complete her secondary education. From 2002, Maria Theresia studied sociology, psychology, and communications in Madrid. Since 2004, she studied communications and media studies with a focus on film and directing in London.

Adulthood

In 2001, Maria Theresia was granted compensation from the Bauer Media Group (German: *Bauer Verlagsgruppe*) upon her appeal to the Higher Regional Court of Hamburg (German: *Hanseatisches Oberlandesgericht*) due to fabricated photograph montages in their *Neue Post* magazine claiming she was to marry Felipe, Prince of Asturias.

Titles, styles, honours and arms

Titles and styles

- **28 November 1980 – present**: *Her Serene Highness* Princess Maria Theresia of Thurn and Taxis

Source (edited): "http://en.wikipedia.org/wiki/Princess_Maria_Theresia_of_Thurn_and_Taxis_(b._1980)"

Princess Mathilde Sophie of Oettingen-Oettingen and Oettingen-Spielberg

Princess Mathilde Sophie of Oettingen-Oettingen and Oettingen-Spielberg (in German: *Mathilde Sophie, Prinzessin zu Oettingen-Oettingen und Oettingen-Spielberg*; 9 February 1816, Oettingen, Kingdom of Bavaria–20 January 1886, Obermais, Meran, County of Tyrol, Austria–Hungary) was a member of the Princely House of Oettingen-Spielberg and a Princess of Oettingen-Oettingen and Oettingen-Spielberg by birth. Through her marriage to Maximilian Karl, 6th Prince of Thurn and Taxis, Mathilde Sophie was also a member of the Princely House of Thurn and Taxis and Princess consort of Thurn and Taxis.

Family

Mathilde Sophie was the eldest daughter and second-eldest child of Johannes Aloysius III, Prince of Oettingen-Oettingen and Oettingen-Spielberg and his wife Princess Amalie Auguste of Wrede.

Marriage and issue

Mathilde Sophie and Maximilian Karl with their family at the occasion of their silver wedding anniversary on 24 January 1864.

Mathilde Sophie married Maximilian Karl, 6th Prince of Thurn and Taxis, fourth child of Karl Alexander, 5th Prince of Thurn and Taxis and his wife Duchess Therese of Mecklenburg-Strelitz, on 24 January 1839 in Oettingen, Kingdom of Bavaria. Mathilde Sophie and Maximilian Karl had twelve children:
- Prince Otto of Thurn and Taxis (28 May 1840 – 6 July 1876)
- Prince Georg of Thurn and Taxis (11 July 1841 – 22 December 1874)
- Prince Paul of Thurn and Taxis (27 May 1843 – 10 March 1879)
- Princess Amalie of Thurn and Taxis (12 May 1844 – 12 February 1867)
- Prince Hugo of Thurn and Taxis (24 November 1845 – 15 May 1873)
- Prince Gustav of Thurn and Taxis (23 February 1848 – 9 July 1914)
- Prince Wilhelm of Thurn and Taxis (20 February 1849 – 11 December 1849)
- Prince Adolf of Thurn and Taxis (26 May 1850 – 3 January 1890)
- Prince Franz of Thurn and Taxis (2 March 1852 – 4 May 1897)
- Prince Nikolaus of Thurn and Taxis (2 August 1853 – 26 May 1874)
- Prince Alfred of Thurn and Taxis (11 June 1856 – 9 February 1886)
- Princess Marie Georgine of Thurn and Taxis (25 December 1857 – 13 February 1909)

Titles and styles
- **9 February 1816 – 24 January 1839**: *Her Serene Highness* Princess Mathilde Sophie of Oettingen-Oettingen and Oettingen-Spielberg
- **24 January 1839 – 10 November 1871**: *Her Serene Highness* The Princess of Thurn and Taxis
- **10 November 1871 – 20 January 1886**: *Her Serene Highness* The Dowager Princess of Thurn and Taxis

Source (edited): "http://en.wikipedia.org/wiki/Princess_Mathilde_Sophie_of_Oettingen-Oettingen_and_Oettingen-Spielberg"

Princess Sophie Friederike of Thurn and Taxis

Princess *Sophie Friederike* Dorothea Henriette of Thurn and Taxis, full German name: *Sophie Friederike Dorothea Henriette, Prinzessin von Thurn und Taxis* (born 20 July 1758 in Regensburg, Free Imperial City of Regensburg, Holy Roman Empire; died 31 May 1800) was a member of the House of Thurn and Taxis and a Princess of Thurn and Taxis by birth and a member of the House of Radziwiłł and Princess Radziwiłł through her marriage to Prince Hieronim Wincenty Radziwiłł. Sophie Friederike was briefly a member of the Kazanowski and Ostroróg Polish noble families through subsequent marriages. She was known as "the Jewel of Regensburg."

Family
Sophie Friederike was the second child and daughter of Karl Anselm, 4th Prince of Thurn and Taxis and his wife Duchess Auguste of Württemberg. She was an elder sister of Karl Alexander, 5th Prince of Thurn and Taxis.

Marriage and issue
Sophie Friederike married Prince Hieronim Wincenty Radziwiłł, son of Michał Kazimierz "Rybeńko" Radziwiłł and his wife Anna Luiza Mycielska, on 31 December 1775 in Regensburg, Free Imperial City of Regensburg, Holy Roman Empire. Sophie Friederike and Hieronim Wincenty had one son:
- Prince Dominik Hieronim Radziwiłł (4 August 1786 – 11 November 1813)

Sophie Friederike married for a second time to a Prince Kazanowski around 1795 and for a third time to a Count Ostroróg around 1797.

Titles, styles, honours and arms

Titles and styles
- **20 July 1758 – 31 December 1775**: *Her Serene Highness* Princess Sophie Friederike of Thurn and Taxis
- **31 December 1775 – c. 1795**: *Her Serene Highness* Princess Sophie Friederike Radziwiłł, Princess of Thurn and Taxis
- **c. 1795 – c. 1797**: *Her Serene Highness* Princess Sophie Friederike Kazanowski, Princess of Thurn and Taxis
- **c. 1797 – 31 May 1800**: *Her Serene Highness* Countess Sophie Friederike Ostroróg, Princess of Thurn and Taxis

Source (edited): "http://en.wikipedia.org/wiki/Princess_Sophie_Friederike_of_Thurn_and_Taxis"

Raimundo, 2nd Duke of Castel Duino

Raimundo, Prince della Torre e Tasso, 2nd Duke of Castel Duino (16 March 1907 – 17 March 1986) was the son of Alessandro, 1st Duke of Castel Duino and Princess Marie of Ligne.

Duke of Castel Duino

His father was naturalised in Italy in 1923 with the title *Prince della Torre e Tasso* and was also created *Duke of Castel Duino*. Raimundo succeeded as 2nd Duke of Castel Duino following the death of his father on 11 March 1937.

Marriage and issue

He was married to Princess Eugénie of Greece and Denmark on 28 November 1949 in Athens. They divorced on 11 May 1965 having had one son who succeeded Raimundo as the 3rd Duke of Castel Duino.

- Carlo Alessandro, 3rd Duke of Castel Duino (born 1952)

Titles, styles, honours and arms

Titles and styles

- **16 March 1907 – 1923**: *His Serene Highness* Prince Raymundo of Thurn and Taxis
- **1923 – 11 March 1937**: *His Serene Highness* Prince Raymundo della Torre e Tasso
- **11 March 1937 – 17 March 1986**: *His Serene Highness* The Duke of Castel Duino

Source (edited): "http://en.wikipedia.org/wiki/Raimundo,_2nd_Duke_of_Castel_Duino"

Thurn-und-Taxis-Post

Carl Jügel's map of the postal and transportation networks in Germany, 1843

Deutsche Bundespost 1984 stamp commemorating the Kaiserlichen Taxis'schen Post

Karl Alexander, 4th Prince of Thurn and Taxis, 1827

The **Thurn-und-Taxis-Post** was a private company and the successor to the Imperial Reichspost of the Holy Roman Empire. The Thurn-und-Taxis-Post was operated by the Princely House of Thurn and Taxis between 1806 and 1867. The company was headquartered in Regensburg from its creation in 1806 until 1810 when it relocated to Frankfurt am Main where it remained until 1867.

The end of the Imperial Reichspost

Throughout the course of the 16th century, the Taxis dynasty was entrusted as the imperial courier of the Holy Roman Empire and in the Spanish Netherlands, Spain, and Burgundy. In 1595, Leonhard I von Taxis was the empire's Postmaster General. Beginning in 1615, the office of Postmaster General of the Imperial Reichspost became hereditary under Lamoral I von Taxis. In 1650, the house was permitted with imperial authorization to rename itself from the *House of Tassis (Taxis)* to the *House of Thurn and Taxis*. As a result, it was able to maintain the Imperial Reichspost in competition with Europe's post offices.

Due to the French Revolutionary Wars and the Napoleonic Wars, the Imperial Reichspost gradually lost more and more postal districts during the tenure of Karl Anselm, 4th Prince of Thurn and Taxis, beginning with the Austrian Netherlands, thus depriving the post of important sources of revenue. Upon the death of Karl Anselm on 13 November 1805, the office of Postmaster General was inherited by his son, Karl Alexander, 5th Prince of Thurn and Taxis.

After the Peace of Pressburg in December 1805, the operation of the Imperial Reichspost of the Holy Roman

Empire was abolished in Württemberg, which then continued under government control. By contrast, Karl Alexander was granted the postal system in the Kingdom of Bavaria as a fiefdom of the House of Thurn and Taxis on 24 February 1806. On 2 May 1806, an agreement was signed between Karl Alexander and the Grand Duchy of Baden, also instituting its postal system as fiefdom of the House of Thurn and Taxis.

The creation of the Confederation of the Rhine on 12 July 1806 virtually meant the end of the Holy Roman Empire and thus the end of the Imperial Reichspost and the hereditary office of Postmaster General held by the of House of Thurn and Taxis. On 6 August 1806, Francis II, Holy Roman Emperor dissolved the empire after the disastrous defeat of the Third Coalition by Napoleon I of France at the Battle of Austerlitz.

While the Imperial Reichspost and the office of Postmaster General ceased to exist, Karl Alexander's wife Therese, Princess of Thurn and Taxis was instrumental in negotiating postal agreements with the Confederation of the Rhine and Napoleon, thus preserving the House of Thurn and Taxis postal monopoly as a private company.

Thurn-und-Taxis-Post

Deutsche Bundespost 1952 stamp depicting a Thurn-und-Taxis-Post cariole

On 1 August 1808, the Kingdom of Bavaria placed the postal system under its government's control. The Grand Duchy of Baden followed suit on 2 August 1811. After Karl Theodor Anton Maria von Dalberg ceded Regensburg to Bavaria in 1810, the House of Thurn and Taxis relocated the headquarters of its postal operations to Frankfurt am Main. After the defeat and exile of Napoleon, the Congress of Vienna recognized the postal claims of the House of Thurn and Taxis in several member states of the German Confederation as legitimate. This recognition resulted in Article 17 of the German Federal Act of 8 June 1815 which required states that had established their own postal system, or intended to do so, to give the House of Thurn and Taxis fair compensation for its loss of revenue.

Under the German Federal Act, the postal systems of the Grand Duchy of Hesse, the duchies of Nassau, Saxe-Weimar, Saxe-Meiningen, and Saxe-Coburg and Gotha, the principalities of Reuss and Schwarzburg-Rudolstadt, the free cities of Frankfurt am Main, Hamburg, Bremen, and Lübeck, the principalities of Hohenzollern-Hechingen, Hohenzollern-Sigmaringen, Lippe-Detmold and Schaumburg-Lippe were placed under the now privately-operated Thurn-und-Taxis-Post. The seat of the post's headquarters in Frankfurt am Main was confirmed on 20 May 1816.

On 14 May 1816, Karl Alexander entered into a contract with William I, Elector of Hesse to operate the postal system of Hesse-Kassel. Prior to the contract, the Thurn-und-Taxis Post had a 23 January 1814 mutual transportation agreement with Hesse-Kassel's state postal system. On 27 July 1819, the Kingdom of Württemberg transferred the ownership and management of its state postal system to the Thurn-und-Taxis-Post due to its inability to pay its compensation owed to the House of Thurn and Taxis.

German-Austrian Postal Association

Thurn-und-Taxis-Post's 1859 15 Kreuzer stamp

In 1847, a German postal conference met in Dresden which resulted in the establishment of the German-Austrian Postal Association. The association came into force on 1 July 1850. On 6 April 1850, the Thurn-und-Taxis-Post joined the German-Austrian Postal Association, which was greeted with negative reactions from the government of the Kingdom of Prussia. Above all, Otto von Bismarck, as a representative of the German Confederation in Frankfurt am Main, was disparaged.

Beginning on 1 January 1852, the Thurn-und-Taxis-Post postage stamp was available in two variants: Kreuzer and Groschen.

The end of the Thurn-und-Taxis-Post

After the Prussian victory in the Austro-Prussian War, the Prussians occupied the Free City of Frankfurt and the Thurn-und-Taxis-Post's headquarters. The Thurn-und-Taxis-Post transferred its postal system contracts to the Prussian state at a fair price after a contract was signed and ratified on 28 January 1867. The handover of control of the postal system took place on 1 July 1867. The last Post Director General of the Thurn-und-Taxis-Post in Frankfurt was Eduard von Schele zu Schelenburg.

Source (edited): "http://en.wikipedia.org/wiki/Thurn-und-Taxis-Post"

Thurn und Taxis

Coat of arms of the princes of Thurn and Taxis, Palais Thurn und Taxis, Frankfurt

The Princely House of **Thurn and Taxis** (German: *das Fürstenhaus Thurn und Taxis*) is a German family that was a key player in the postal services in Europe in the 16th century and is well known as owners of breweries and builders of many castles.

History

In the 12th century, the Lombardic family Tasso (meaning Badger or collector) was resident in the mountain village of Cornello now *Cornello dei Tasso* near Bergamo in Val Brembana. The translation of "Tasso" to German: *Dachs* was the origin of the name "Taxis", and the badger is still represented in the family coat of arms. In 1624 the family became counts (*Grafen*). In 1650 they changed their name to Thurn (= Turm = Tower) und Taxis. In 1695 they received their princely title from Holy Roman Emperor Leopold I.

Rainer Maria Rilke wrote his *Duino Elegies* while visiting Princess Marie of Thurn and Taxis (*née* princess of Hohenlohe) at her family's Duino castle. Rilke later dedicated his only novel *The Notebooks of Malte Laurids Brigge* to the princess, who was his patroness. Marie's relation to Regensburg's Thurn and Taxis is rather distant, however; she was married to Alexander Thurn and Taxis, a member of the family's branch that in the early 19th century settled in Bohemia (now Czech Republic) and became strongly connected to Czech national culture and history.

Several members of the family have been Knights of Malta.

The current head of the house of Thurn and Taxis is HSH Albert II, 12th Prince of Thurn and Taxis, son of Johannes and his wife, Gloria. The family is one of the wealthiest in Germany. The family has resided in St. Emmeram Castle in Regensburg since 1748. The family's brewery was sold to the Paulaner Group (Munich) in 1996, but still produces beer under the brand of Thurn und Taxis.

Ruggiano de Tassis founded a postal service in Italy. And later in Innsbruck, on 11 December 1489, Jeannetto de Tassis was appointed Chief Master of Postal Services. The family held its exclusive position for centuries. On 12 November 1516 the Taxis family had a postal service based in Brussels — where the eponymous extensive warehouse and railway goods yard complex is currently under development as a cultural centre — reaching to Rome, Naples, Spain, Germany and France by courier.

The Thurn und Taxis company would last until the 18th century, when the postal service was finally bought by the heir to the Spanish throne.

- Eugen Alexander Franz (1695–1714)
- Anselm Franz (1714–1739)
- Alexander Ferdinand (1739–1773)
- Karl Anselm (1773–1805)
- Karl Alexander (1805–1827)
- Maximilian Karl (1827–1871)
- Maximilian Maria (1871–1885)
- Albert I (1885–1952)
- Franz Joseph (1952–1971)
- Karl August (1971–1982)
- Johannes (1982–1990)
- Albert II (1990-)

The Thurn and Taxis family came to massive media attention during the late-1970s through mid-1980s when late Prince Johannes married Countess Mariae Gloria of Schönburg-Glauchau, a member of an impoverished noble family. The couple's wild, "jet set" lifestyle and Princess Gloria's over-the-top appearance (characterized by bright hair color and flashy clothes) earned her the nickname Princess TNT.

Source (edited): "http://en.wikipedia.org/wiki/Thurn_und_Taxis"